Food Foraging Secrets of Our Ancestors

Discover How to Confidently Identify, Harvest and Cook Nature's Edible Plants & More.

NOTICE: You <u>Do NOT</u> Have the Right to Reprint or Resell this Report

Disclaimer

The identification and use or ingestion of wild plants requires caution and diligence. Never consume any plant unless you are positive it is safe to eat. Before harvesting any of the plants discussed in this book, please take the time to thoroughly read the introduction to wild edibles. This book is intended for educational purposes only and should not be relied upon as a substitute for medical advice, diagnosis, or treatment. The author, publisher, and any other parties involved cannot be held responsible for any negative effects experienced by the reader. Due to food allergies, it is possible for an individual to have a reaction to a plant that is typically considered safe. By choosing to consume unfamiliar foods, the reader assumes all risks and responsibilities. Please exercise caution when harvesting wild edibles.

In the world of foraging, nothing is ever guaranteed. The topic of wild edibles is a controversial one, with many differing expert opinions. This book may present viewpoints that are not in agreement with others in the field. The information in this book is based on the author's extensive research and personal experience, but it is ultimately just their opinion. The author encourages readers to question their information and create their own protocol for foraging. There are inherent risks associated with harvesting and eating wild foods, but the benefits of incorporating nature's bounty into one's lifestyle far outweigh the dangers. The author supports readers who wish to integrate wild edibles into their lifestyle and stands by the message in this book.

INTRODUCTION

For centuries, our ancestors relied on foraging as a means of survival. They knew how to identify safe wild plants, trees, and vegetation to eat, and how to prepare it for consumption. In this book, we will delve into the secrets of our ancestors and uncover their knowledge on foraging.

In today's world, many people have become detached from the natural world and the idea of foraging for food may seem foreign. However, with the increasing threat of natural disasters and economic uncertainty, it is becoming more important than ever to have the skills and knowledge to provide for oneself and one's family. Foraging is not only a means of survival, but it also offers a connection to the earth and a sense of self-reliance.

However, it is important to exercise caution when foraging. Eating the wrong plant can have serious consequences, and even plants that are safe can be toxic if prepared incorrectly. This book will provide you with the tools and knowledge to safely and confidently forage for wild edibles.

From identifying safe plants to preparation techniques, this book covers everything you need to know about foraging. Whether you are a seasoned forager or just starting out, this book will provide valuable information and insights that will deepen your understanding of the art and science of foraging.

So, join us on a journey to rediscover the foraging secrets of our ancestors, and learn how to provide for yourself and your family in the most natural and sustainable way possible.

KNOW YOUR REGION:

One of the most important aspects of foraging is understanding the plants and vegetation in your region. Different regions have different ecosystems, and the plants that grow in one area may not be found in another. It is crucial to familiarize yourself with the plants in your area so that you can confidently identify which ones are safe to eat and which ones should be avoided.

Knowing your region will also help you to recognize the seasonal availability of different plants. For example, some plants may only be available in the spring or fall, while others may grow year-round. Understanding the seasonal availability of plants will help you to plan your foraging trips and make the most of the resources available to you.

It is also important to be aware of any dangers or hazards in your region, such as poisonous plants or animals, so that you can take the necessary precautions. For example, in some regions, there may be plants that are safe to eat, but have toxic look-alikes that can be easily mistaken. In these cases, it is essential to have a reliable guide or reference to help you identify the plants correctly.

UNIVERSAL EDIBILITY TEST:

In a survival situation, it is important to be able to identify which plants, trees, and flowers are safe to eat. When you are unsure, you can use the Universal Edibility Test to determine if a plant is safe. This test is a simple and effective way to determine the edibility of a plant, and has been used by foragers and survivalists for generations.

Here's how to perform the Universal Edibility Test:

1. Start by selecting a small portion of the plant that you want to test. This should include leaves, stems, and any other parts that you are considering eating.
2. Rub a small portion of the plant on the inside of your wrist or forearm. Wait for 15 minutes to see if there is any skin irritation or allergic reaction.
3. Place a small portion of the plant on your tongue and hold it there for 15 minutes. Do not swallow. Observe for any mouth or tongue irritation.
4. If there are no skin or mouth irritations, you can proceed to the next step. Cook a small portion of the plant and wait for 8 hours.
5. If there are no symptoms after 8 hours, such as stomach discomfort or headaches, you can eat a small portion of the cooked plant. Observe yourself for another 8 hours.
6. If there are no symptoms after the second 8 hours, the plant can be considered safe to eat.

It is important to note that the Universal Edibility Test is not foolproof and there is still a small chance of having an adverse reaction to a plant that has passed the test. However, it is a useful skill to know and can help you to make informed decisions when you are unsure of a plant's edibility.

POISONOUS PLANTS & INSECTS TO AVOID:

While foraging can be a great way to obtain safe and nutritious food, it is important to be aware of poisonous plants that you should avoid. Some plants are so toxic they can be deadly if consumed

If you come into contact with or ingest any of the following, it is important to seek medical attention as soon as possible. Avoid consuming these plants, as their toxic compounds can cause serious symptoms, including nausea, rash, vomiting, and even death.

Here are a few of the most encountered poisonous plants to avoid:

POISON IVY, POISON OAK, AND POISON SUMAC

Three of the most encountered poisonous plants are poison ivy, poison oak, and poison sumac. These contain an oil called urushiol that can cause an itchy and painful rash if it meets your skin.

Poison ivy is a common plant found throughout North America. It is easily recognizable by its three leaves that grow in a cluster and its red stems. The leaves can vary in shape and size, but they always grow in groups of three. In the spring, poison ivy produces small, green flowers. In the fall it produces small, white berries.

Poison oak is found primarily in the western United States. It is similar in appearance to poison ivy, but it has leaves that grow in groups of three or five and are more lobed. In the spring, poison oak produces yellow or green flowers, and in the fall, it produces small, white berries.

Poison sumac is found primarily in the eastern United States. It is a small tree or shrub that has leaves that grow in groups of seven to thirteen. The leaves of poison sumac are shiny and green, and they turn red in the fall. In the spring, poison sumac produces small, green flowers, and in the fall, it produces small, white berries.

NIGHTSHADE

Nightshade is a family of plants that includes several species that are poisonous to humans, such as deadly nightshade and black nightshade. These contain toxic compounds that can cause serious symptoms, including hallucinations, confusion, and even death.

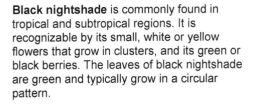

Deadly nightshade is commonly found in Europe and North America. It is recognizable by its small, bell-shaped flowers that are typically purple or blue, and its shiny, black berries. The leaves of deadly nightshade are green and shiny, and grow in a circular pattern.

Black nightshade is commonly found in tropical and subtropical regions. It is recognizable by its small, white or yellow flowers that grow in clusters, and its green or black berries. The leaves of black nightshade are green and typically grow in a circular pattern.

JIMSONWEED

Jimsonweed is a poisonous plant that is commonly found in the southern United States. It is recognizable by its large, trumpet-shaped flowers that are typically white or purple, and its prickly leaves. Jimsonweed contains toxic compounds that can cause serious symptoms, including hallucinations, confusion, and even death.

Leaves of jimsonweed are green and grow in a circular pattern. The plant typically grows to be several feet tall with a prickly stem.

WATER HEMLOCK

Water hemlock is a poisonous plant that is found near bodies of water. It is recognizable by its green stems and its small, white flowers that grow in clusters. Water hemlock contains toxic compounds that can cause serious symptoms, including seizures, convulsions, and death.

The leaves of water hemlock are green and typically grow in a circular pattern. The plant typically grows to be several feet tall and has a smooth stem.

YEW

Yew is a poisonous plant that is commonly found in temperate regions. It is recognizable by its red berries and its evergreen needles. Yew contains toxic compounds that can cause serious symptoms, including nausea, vomiting, and even death.

The needles of yew are dark green and grow in a spiral pattern. The plant typically grows to be several feet tall and has a smooth stem.

BANEBERRY

Baneberry is a poisonous plant that is commonly found in North America and Europe. It is recognizable by its small, white or red berries and its fern-like leaves. Baneberry contains toxic compounds that can cause serious symptoms, including nausea, vomiting, and even death.

The leaves of baneberry are green and typically grow in a circular pattern. The plant typically grows to be several feet tall and has a smooth stem.

BUTTERCUP

Buttercup is a poisonous plant that is commonly found in North America and Europe. It is recognizable by its bright yellow or orange flowers and its leaves that grow in a circular pattern. Buttercup contains toxic compounds that can cause serious symptoms, including skin irritation, stomach pain, and even death.

The plant grows to be several inches tall and has a smooth stem.

DEATH CAMAS

Death camas is a poisonous plant that is commonly found in western North America. It is recognizable by its small, white or yellow flowers that grow in clusters and its leaves that grow in a basal rosette. Death camas contains toxic compounds that can cause serious symptoms, including nausea, vomiting, and even death.

The leaves of death camas are long and narrow, and they are typically blue-green in color. The plant typically grows to be several inches tall and has a smooth stem.

FALSE HELLEBORE

False hellebore is a poisonous plant that is commonly found in North America and Europe. It is recognizable by its green or yellow flowers that grow in clusters and its leaves that grow in a basal rosette. False hellebore contains toxic compounds that can cause serious symptoms, including nausea, vomiting, and even death.

The leaves of false hellebore are long and narrow, and they are typically green in color. The plant typically grows to be several feet tall and has a smooth stem.

FOXGLOVE

Foxglove is a poisonous plant that is commonly found in North America and Europe. It is recognizable by its tall spikes of bell-shaped flowers that are typically purple, pink, or white. Foxglove contains toxic compounds that can cause serious symptoms, including nausea, vomiting, heart problems, and even death.

The leaves of foxglove are green and typically grow in a basal rosette. The plant typically grows to be several feet tall and has a smooth stem.

LUPINE

Lupine is a poisonous plant that is commonly found in North America and Europe. It is recognizable by its spikes of colorful flowers that come in a variety of colors, including blue, purple, pink, and yellow. Lupine contains toxic compounds that can cause serious symptoms, including nausea, vomiting, and even death.

The leaves of lupine are green and typically grow in a basal rosette. The plant typically grows to be several feet tall and has a smooth stem.

10 INSECTS TO NEVER EAT

1. **Monarch butterfly**: The monarch butterfly and its larvae contain toxic chemicals that can cause nausea, vomiting, and other health problems.

2. **Ladybug**: While some species of ladybugs are safe to eat, others can secrete a toxic substance that can cause illness.

3. **Firefly**: Fireflies contain a toxic chemical called lucibufagins, which can cause vomiting, convulsions, and even death if ingested.

4. **Housefly**: Houseflies can carry a variety of bacteria and parasites that can cause illness if ingested.

5. **Cockroach**: Cockroaches can carry a variety of bacteria and parasites that can cause illness if ingested.

6. **Caterpillars** with spiky hairs: Some caterpillars have spiky hairs that can cause skin irritation or even an allergic reaction if ingested.

7. **Bees and wasps**: While honeybees and bumblebees are generally safe to eat in small quantities, wasps and hornets can cause allergic reactions and should not be consumed.

8. **Centipedes**: Centipedes can be toxic and cause pain and swelling if ingested.

9. **Spiders**: While some species of spiders are safe to eat, others can be toxic and cause illness or even death.

10. **Ticks**: Ticks can carry a variety of diseases and should not be consumed.

FORAGING FOR FOOD

In this section we will go over many plants, trees and other vegetation that are safe to eat when foraging for food.

ACORNS

Acorns are the nuts of oak trees and are a commonly foraged food source in many parts of the world, including North America. They are a staple food for many indigenous cultures and have been used for centuries as a source of nutrition and sustenance.

Acorns are easily identified by their distinctive, nut-like appearance and by the oak tree they come from. They are typically harvested in the fall, when they have fully matured and fallen from the tree.

Acorns grow on a variety of oak trees, including red oak and white oak, and are commonly found in forests, woodlands, and along the edges of fields and meadows. They are a hardy plant that is well-suited to a wide range of growing conditions.

Harvesting acorns requires some preparation, as they contain tannins that are toxic to humans and must be removed before they can be consumed. This typically involves soaking the acorns in water to leach out the tannins, and then grinding them into a flour-like consistency that can be used in a variety of dishes.

Acorns are a nutritious food source rich in carbohydrates, fiber, and vitamins and minerals, including vitamins B and E and minerals like magnesium, potassium, and iron. They are also a good source of healthy fats, including monounsaturated and polyunsaturated fats.

Acorns can be used in a variety of ways, including as a flour in baking and cooking, a thickener in soups and stews, or a substitute for rice or other grains in recipes. They have a slightly nutty flavor and are a versatile ingredient that can be used in a variety of dishes.

ALDER

Alder is a deciduous tree that is commonly found growing along streams, rivers and other bodies of water in temperate climates. It is a versatile and edible plant that can be a valuable food source for those who know how to identify and prepare it.

Alder can be identified by its smooth, gray bark and its small, cone-like fruits that hang from the branches. It blooms in the spring, producing small, inconspicuous flowers that give way to edible fruits later in the season.

When harvesting alder, gather the cones while they are still green and before they have a chance to mature and release their seeds. They can be used fresh or dried for later use, and can be consumed raw or cooked.

Alder is a nutritious plant high in protein and antioxidants, making it a valuable addition to a forager's diet. It is also believed to have anti-inflammatory properties and is beneficial for digestive health.

To prepare alder for eating, the cones can be roasted or boiled until they are soft and the scales can be easily removed. The scales can then be eaten raw, added to soups or stews, or used to make a nutritious tea. Some people also grind the scales into a flour-like powder that can be used as a gluten-free alternative in baking.

ALOE VERA

Aloe vera is a succulent plant that is native to the Arabian Peninsula but has been widely cultivated and naturalized in other parts of the world. It is best known for its medicinal properties, but the gel-like substance inside the leaves is also edible and has a long history of use as a food and tonic.

Aloe vera can be identified by its rosette of large, fleshy leaves that are often marked with white, spiny teeth along the edges. The plant produces tall spikes of yellow or orange flowers that bloom in the summer.

Aloe vera grows in a variety of habitats, including deserts, rocky outcroppings, and coastal regions. When harvesting aloe vera, gather the leaves that are at least one year old and have had a chance to mature. Harvest the leaves by cutting them at the base of the plant, taking care not to damage the plant or other nearby leaves.

Aloe vera is a good source of vitamins, minerals, and antioxidants. It is also rich in dietary fiber, and it has been shown to have anti-inflammatory and digestive health benefits.

The gel-like substance inside the leaves of aloe vera can be used in a variety of ways, including as a base for smoothies, as a thickener in soups and stews, or as a substitute for mayonnaise or cream in recipes. It can also be used topically for skin care or wound healing.

AMARANTH

Amaranth is an annual herb that is native to the Americas, but it has been widely cultivated and naturalized in other parts of the world. It is a highly nutritious plant that has been used for food, medicine, and religious purposes for thousands of years.

Amaranth can be easily identified by its tall, upright growth habit and its long, green or red leaves. It produces clusters of small, green or red flowers that bloom in the summer and are followed by small, grain-like seeds.

Amaranth grows in a variety of habitats, including cultivated fields, waste ground, and roadsides. It is a highly adaptable plant that is well-suited to a wide range of growing conditions and can be found throughout North America.

When harvesting amaranth, it is best to gather the seeds when they are fully mature and have turned from green to a golden or reddish-brown color. The seeds can be harvested by cutting the stems, threshing the seeds, and winnowing to remove the chaff.

Amaranth is a highly nutritious plant that is a good source of protein, fiber, and vitamins and minerals, including iron, calcium, and B vitamins. It is also rich in antioxidants and has been shown to have anti-inflammatory and heart-healthy benefits.

Amaranth can be used in a variety of ways, including as a cereal grain, a thickener in soups and stews, or as a substitute for wheat flour in baking. The seeds can be roasted and popped like popcorn, or they can be ground into flour and used to make porridge, cakes, and other baked goods. The leaves can also be eaten as a leafy green, either raw or cooked.

ASPEN TREE

Aspen is a type of tree that is commonly found in North America and is a valuable resource for foragers looking for food. The young shoots of the aspen tree are edible and have a slightly sweet and tangy flavor, making them a versatile ingredient for a variety of dishes.

Aspen trees are easily recognizable by their distinctive, white bark and rounded leaves that quiver in the wind. They grow in a variety of habitats, including forests, meadows, and along riverbanks, and are often found in areas with moist, well-drained soils.

They are best harvested before the leaves have fully emerged, as the flavor can become more bitter as the shoots mature. To harvest aspen shoots, simply snap off the young shoots near the base of the tree. They can then be washed and used fresh, or they can be dried or preserved for later use.

Aspen shoots are a nutritious food source that are rich in vitamins and minerals, including vitamins A, C, and K, as well as minerals like potassium, calcium, and magnesium. They are also a good source of fiber and antioxidants, making them a healthy addition to any diet.

Aspen shoots can be used in a variety of ways, including as a fresh salad green, as a cooked vegetable, or as an ingredient in soups, stews, and stir-fries. They can also be used to make a delicious tea that is rich in vitamins and minerals.

BEECHNUTS

Beechnuts are the edible nuts produced by the American Beech tree (Fagus grandifolia), which is native to North America. They are small, triangular nuts that are encased in a prickly, green husk and mature in the fall.

Beechnuts can be easily identified by their distinctive, triangular shape and

their husk, which is covered in prickly spikes. The trees are commonly found in forests and along the edges of rivers and streams, and they prefer moist, well-drained soils.

Beechnuts are in season from late summer to early autumn, and they can be harvested by shaking the tree or picking them up from the ground. The nuts have a sweet, nutty flavor and are often roasted or used in baking.

Beechnuts are rich in vitamins and minerals, including vitamins B and E, and minerals such as magnesium and potassium. They are also a good source of healthy unsaturated fats, fiber, and protein.

To prepare beechnuts for eating, it is important to remove the husk and then roast or boil the nuts to remove any bitterness. The nuts can then be eaten as a snack, added to baked goods, or used in cooking. Try using beechnuts in savory dishes such as roasted vegetables or in sweet dishes such as cakes and cookies for a unique and delicious foraging experience!

BLACKBERRY

Blackberry is a perennial shrub that is commonly found in temperate climates and is widely distributed throughout the world. It is a popular foraging plant that is known for its sweet, juicy fruits that are often used in jams, jellies, and baked goods.

Blackberry can be easily identified by its thorny canes, large, lobed leaves, and clusters of small, white or pink flowers that bloom in the spring. The fruits usually ripen in late summer to early fall and are black in color when fully ripe.

Blackberries grow in a variety of habitats, from woodland edges and hedgerows to fields and waste ground. They are often found along roadsides, fences, and other disturbed areas, and they are well adapted to colonizing new areas.

When harvesting blackberries, it is best to pick the fruits when they are fully ripe and have a deep, rich color. They can be harvested by gently pulling the fruit from the cane, taking care not to break the canes or damage the plant.

Blackberries are a nutritious food that is high in vitamins, minerals, and antioxidants. They are also a good source of fiber, and they have been shown to have anti-inflammatory and cardiovascular health benefits.

Blackberries can be eaten raw, cooked, or baked into a variety of dishes. They can be used to make jams, jellies, syrups, and baked goods, or they can be added to smoothies, pies, and other desserts. They can also be dried or frozen for later use.

BLACK LOCUST

Black locust, also known as Robinia pseudoacacia, is a deciduous tree that is native to North America. It produces edible flowers that have been used for food and medicine for centuries.

Black locust can be identified by its distinctive compound leaves, which consist of many small leaflets. The tree produces clusters of fragrant, white

or pink flowers in the late spring or early summer. The flowers are similar in appearance to pea flowers and have a sweet, floral flavor.

Black locust can be found in a variety of habitats, including forests, meadows, and along roadsides. It is a hardy tree that can grow in a variety of soil types and climates.

To harvest black locust flowers, the flower clusters can be carefully picked from the tree by hand. Black locust flowers are a good source of antioxidants and have potential health benefits for the immune system and digestion.

However, it's important to note that other parts of the black locust tree, such as the bark, leaves, and seeds, contain toxic compounds and should not be consumed.

To prepare and eat black locust flowers, they should be washed and can be eaten raw or cooked. They have a sweet, floral flavor that pairs well with other ingredients, such as honey and cheese. Black locust flowers can also be used to make tea or infused into syrups and tinctures for medicinal use.

BIRCH TREE

Birch trees (Betula species) are commonly found in northern hemisphere forests and are a popular source of food for foragers. The bark, leaves, sap, and inner bark of the birch tree are all edible and have a distinctive, slightly sweet flavor.

Birch trees can be identified by their unique, white or silver bark that peels away in paper-like sheets. They have a rounded crown and simple, triangular leaves that are 2-5 inches long. In late spring to early summer, birch trees produce small, pendulous catkins that turn into small, triangular seeds.

The sap from birch trees is a popular food source, and can be collected by tapping the trunk of the tree with a drill and collecting the sap in a bucket. The sap is high in sugars and can be consumed as a sweet drink or used to make birch syrup, a sweet condiment that is similar to maple syrup.

The inner bark of the birch tree is also edible and is a good source of carbohydrates and vitamin C. It can be harvested by carefully peeling away the outer bark to reveal the soft, white inner layer. This inner bark can be dried and ground into a flour, or boiled to make a nutritious tea.

Birch leaves can be brewed into a tea that is high in Vitamin C and antioxidants. They can also be added to salads or used as a seasoning.

BLUEBERRY

Wild blueberries are a low-growing shrub that are native to North America. They are a common and highly valued food source, prized for their sweet, juicy berries that are used in a variety of dishes, including baked goods, jams, jellies, and sauces.

Wild blueberries can be easily identified by their small, deciduous leaves, twiggy branches, and small, white or pink flowers that bloom in the spring.
The berries are typically blue in color and are round, with a powdery coating that gives them a distinctive appearance.

Wild blueberries grow in a variety of habitats, including forests, bogs, and heaths. They are most commonly found in the northeastern and northwestern regions of the United States and in eastern Canada, and they are also widely cultivated for commercial production.

When harvesting wild blueberries, it is best to pick the berries when they are fully ripe and have a deep blue color. The berries can be harvested by gently pinching them from the stem, taking care not to damage the plant or other nearby berries.

Wild blueberries are a highly nutritious food that is a good source of vitamins, minerals, and antioxidants. They are also low in calories and have been shown to have anti-inflammatory, cardiovascular, and brain-health benefits.

Wild blueberries can be eaten raw, cooked, or baked into a variety of dishes. They can be used to make jams, jellies, syrups, and baked goods, or they can be added to smoothies, pies, and other desserts. They can also be dried or frozen for later use.

BURDOCK

Burdock is a biennial plant that is native to Europe and Asia, but it has been widely naturalized in other parts of the world, including North America.

Burdock can be easily identified by its large, dark green leaves that are covered in a velvety down, and its large, purple or pink flowers that bloom in the summer. The plant produces long, spiny burrs that are often a nuisance to people and animals, but the roots are long, fleshy, and edible.

Burdock grows in a variety of habitats, including waste ground, roadsides, and cultivated fields. It is a hardy plant that is well-suited to a wide range of growing conditions and can be found throughout North America.

When harvesting burdock, it is best to gather the roots in the fall or early spring, when they are most tender and flavorful. The roots can be harvested by digging around the base of the plant, taking care not to damage the plant or other nearby roots.

Burdock is a highly nutritious plant and a good source of vitamins, minerals, and dietary fiber. It is also rich in antioxidants and has been shown to have anti-inflammatory and liver-protective benefits.

Burdock can be used in a variety of ways, including as a root vegetable, a thickener in soups and stews, or as a substitute for potatoes or other root vegetables in recipes. The young shoots can also be eaten raw or cooked, and they have a crisp, crunchy texture and a slightly bitter flavor.

CAT'S EAR

Cat's ear, also known as False Dandelion or Flatweed, is a wild edible plant commonly found in North America and Europe. It is a low-growing plant with leaves that resemble a cat's ear, hence its name. The leaves are usually a deep green color and have a slightly bitter taste.

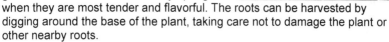

Cat's ear grows in a variety of environments, including grassy fields, roadsides, and gardens. It is in bloom in the spring and summer months and produces yellow flowers that resemble those of a dandelion.

To harvest cat's ear, pull the leaves from the plant and rinse them thoroughly to remove any dirt or debris. The leaves can be eaten raw or cooked and are often used in salads or as a cooked green.

Cat's ear is a rich source of vitamins and minerals, including vitamins A, C, and K, and minerals such as iron, potassium, and calcium. It is also a good source of antioxidants, which help to protect the body against damage from harmful substances.

When preparing cat's ear, remember that the leaves can be slightly bitter, so they may be better suited to be used in combination with other ingredients in recipes. Ppopular ways to use cat's ear include in soups, stews, and casseroles, or as a cooked green.

CATTAIL

Cattail (Typha latifolia) is a common and widespread aquatic plant that is often used for foraging food. This plant is easy to identify by its long, cylindrical spikes of brown flowers that are surrounded by long, narrow green leaves. The leaves of cattail are often referred to as "flags" because they resemble the flags of a ship.

Cattail grows in shallow, marshy areas and along the edges of ponds, lakes, and rivers. It is a hardy plant that can grow in a variety of conditions, from full sun to partial shade. It is most commonly found in North America and Europe, but can also be found in other parts of the world.

Cattail contains a variety of vitamins and minerals, including vitamins A, C, and E, and potassium, phosphorus, and magnesium. It is also a good source of fiber and protein, making it a nutritious food source for foragers.

To harvest cattail, simply snap off the young shoots at the base of the plant or cut the brown spikes of flowers just above the leaves. The young shoots can be eaten raw or cooked, while the spikes of flowers can be roasted and ground into flour. The leaves can also be used to wrap food for cooking, much like a corn husk.

When preparing cattail, it is important to wash it thoroughly to remove any dirt or debris. The young shoots can be boiled or steamed, while the spikes of flowers can be roasted or ground into flour. The leaves can also be used to wrap food for cooking, much like a corn husk. Try cattail in soups, stews, stir-fries, or as a side dish for a unique and nutritious foraging experience!

CEDAR

Cedar trees (Cedrus spp.) are coniferous trees commonly found in many parts of the world, including North America, Europe, and Asia. They are known for their distinctive, fragrant wood, which is often used for building homes, furniture, and other structures.

Cedar trees can be identified by their tall, straight trunk and the characteristic "cedar smell" of their wood. They have needles that grow in clusters and are typically blue-green in color. Cedar trees are also known for their cones, which are large and cone-shaped.

Cedar trees grow in a variety of habitats, including forests, mountains, and along rivers. They can tolerate a wide range of soils and climates, making them a versatile and widespread species.

Cedar trees are not typically used for foraging food, as their needles and cones are not commonly consumed by humans. However, the inner bark of the tree can be eaten in times of food scarcity.

To harvest the inner bark of a cedar tree, first locate a healthy tree with a thick trunk. Then, use a knife to carefully peel away the outer bark and reveal the inner bark.

Cedar trees are not a significant source of vitamins or minerals, but they do contain some nutrients and have been used for medicinal purposes for centuries. The inner bark is high in carbohydrates and can provide a source of energy.

When preparing cedar bark for eating, it is important to clean it thoroughly and remove any dirt or debris. The inner bark can be eaten raw or cooked, and it can be boiled, roasted, or dried for later use. Try adding cedar bark to soups, stews, or as a side dish for a unique and nutritious foraging experience!

CHESTNUTS

Chestnuts are the edible nuts produced by the chestnut tree (Castanea spp.), which is native to Europe, Asia, and North America. They are large, round nuts that are encased in a prickly, green husk and mature in the fall.

Chestnuts can be easily identified by their large, round shape and their husk, which is covered in prickly spikes. The trees are commonly found in forests and along the edges of rivers and streams, and they prefer moist, well-drained soils.

Chestnuts are in season from late summer to autumn, and can be harvested by shaking the tree or picking them up from the ground.

Chestnuts are rich in vitamins and minerals, including vitamins C and B6, and minerals such as magnesium and potassium. They are also a good source of healthy unsaturated fats, fiber, and protein.

To prepare chestnuts for eating, it is important to remove the husk and then roast or boil the nuts to remove any bitterness. The nuts can then be eaten as a snack, added to baked goods, or used in cooking. Try using chestnuts in savory dishes such as roasted vegetables or in sweet dishes such as cakes and cookies for a unique and delicious foraging experience!

CHICKWEED

Chickweed (Stellaria media) is a small, annual herb that is commonly found in many parts of the world, including North America, Europe, and Asia.

Chickweed can be easily identified by its small, white flowers and its small, oval-shaped leaves. The leaves are smooth and have a slightly glossy appearance, and they are attached to delicate stems that often trail along the ground. It has a mild, slightly sweet flavor similar to spinach.

Chickweed grows in a variety of habitats, including fields, gardens, and along forest edges. It is often found in disturbed soils, such as along the sides of roads and in fields that were recently tilled.

Chickweed is in bloom from spring to early summer, and the leaves and stems are edible during this time. The plant is rich in vitamins and minerals, including vitamins A and C, and calcium, iron, and potassium. Chickweed is also a good source of fiber and protein, making it a nutritious food source for foragers.

To harvest chickweed, simply cut the stems and leaves from the plant. Be sure to only harvest chickweed from areas that have not been treated with pesticides or other chemicals.

When preparing chickweed for eating, it is important to wash it thoroughly to remove any dirt or debris. The plant can be eaten raw or cooked, and it can be boiled, steamed, or sautéed for a nutritious and delicious side dish. Try using chickweed in a salad with other wild greens, or as a topping for soups or stews for a unique and nutritious foraging experience!

CHICORY

Chicory is a perennial herb that is native to Europe and Asia, but it has been widely naturalized in other parts of the world, including North America.

Chicory can be easily identified by its tall, upright growth habit and its large, lobed leaves that are blue-green in color. The plant produces bright blue or purple flowers that bloom in the summer and are followed by small achenes (seeds) that are surrounded by a tuft of white hair.

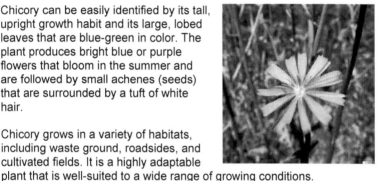

Chicory grows in a variety of habitats, including waste ground, roadsides, and cultivated fields. It is a highly adaptable plant that is well-suited to a wide range of growing conditions.

When harvesting chicory, it is best to gather the leaves when they are young and tender, before the plant begins to flower. The leaves can be harvested by cutting or breaking them from the plant, taking care not to damage the plant or other nearby leaves.

Chicory is a highly nutritious plant that is a good source of vitamins, minerals, and antioxidants. It is also rich in dietary fiber, and it has been shown to have anti-inflammatory and digestive health benefits.

Chicory can be used in a variety of ways, including as a leafy green, a substitute for lettuce in salads, or as a cooked green, similar to spinach or kale. The roots can be roasted and ground to make coffee substitute, and the young shoots can be pickled or added to salads.

CHOKECHERRY

Chokecherry is a deciduous shrub that is native to North America. It is a highly valued food source, prized for its tart, juicy berries that are used in a variety of dishes, including jams, jellies, syrups, and baked goods.

Chokecherry can be identified by its tall, shrubby growth habit, its leaves that are dark green and glossy on the top and lighter green and fuzzy on the bottom, and its clusters of small, white or pink flowers that bloom in the spring. The berries are black or dark red in color and are round, with a distinctive tart flavor.

Chokecherry grows in a variety of habitats, including forests, stream banks, and rocky outcroppings. It is a hardy plant suited to a wide range of growing conditions and found throughout North America.

When harvesting chokecherries, it is best to pick the berries when they are fully ripe and have a deep, dark color. The berries can be harvested by gently pinching them from the stem, taking care not to damage the plant or other nearby berries.

Chokecherries are a highly nutritious food that is a good source of vitamins, minerals, and antioxidants. They are also low in calories and have been shown to have anti-inflammatory, cardiovascular, and brain-health benefits.

Chokecherries can be eaten raw, cooked, or baked into a variety of dishes. They can be used to make jams, jellies, syrups, and baked goods, or they can be added to pies, sauces, and other desserts. They can also be dried or frozen for later use.

CLOVER

Clover (Trifolium spp.) is a common and widespread plant that is often used for foraging food. It is a member of the pea family and is easily recognized by its distinctive, trifoliate leaves and its small, round flowers, which are typically pink, white, or red.

Clover grows in a variety of habitats, including fields, meadows, and along the edges of forests. It is a hardy plant that can grow in a variety of conditions, from full sun to partial shade. Clover is most commonly found in North America, Europe, and Asia.

Clover is in bloom from spring to early summer, and the flowers and leaves are edible during this time. The plant is rich in vitamins and minerals, including vitamins A, C, and K, and iron, calcium, and potassium. Clover is also a good source of fiber and protein.

To harvest clover, simply cut the stems and leaves from the plant. Be sure to only harvest clover from areas that have not been treated with pesticides or other chemicals.

When preparing clover for eating, it is important to wash it thoroughly to remove any dirt or debris. The plant can be eaten raw or cooked, and it can be boiled, steamed, or sautéed for a nutritious and delicious side dish. Try using clover in a salad with other wild greens, or as a topping for soups or stews.

COMMON MALLOW

Common Mallow (Malva neglecta) is an herbaceous plant that is commonly found in many parts of the world, including North America, Europe, and Asia. It is a hardy plant that grows in a variety of habitats, including fields, meadows, and along the edges of forests.

Common Mallow can be easily identified by its large, round leaves and its small, pink, white, or purple flowers, which grow in clusters. The plant has a distinctive, slightly mucilaginous texture, and its leaves and flowers are edible.

Common Mallow is in bloom from spring to early autumn, and the leaves and flowers are edible during this time. The plant is rich in vitamins and minerals, including vitamins A, C, and K, and calcium, iron, and potassium. Common Mallow is also a good source of fiber and protein, making it a nutritious food source for foragers.

To harvest Common Mallow, simply cut the stems and leaves from the plant. Be sure to only harvest Common Mallow from areas that have not been treated with pesticides or other chemicals.

When preparing Common Mallow for eating, it is important to wash it thoroughly to remove any dirt or debris. The plant can be eaten raw or cooked, and it can be boiled, steamed, or sautéed for a nutritious and delicious side dish. Try using Common Mallow in a salad with other wild greens, or as a topping for soups or stews for a unique and nutritious foraging experience.

CURLY DOCK

Curly dock, also known as Rumex crispus, is a perennial plant that is commonly found in North America, Europe, and Asia. It is an edible plant that has been used for food and medicine for centuries.

Curly dock can be identified by its distinctive curly leaves, which are green and grow in a rosette pattern. The plant produces tall, slender flower stalks in the summer, which are topped with clusters of small, greenish flowers. The plant also produces long, slender seeds that turn reddish-brown when mature.

Curly dock is a hardy plant that can grow in a variety of habitats, including fields, meadows, and along roadsides. It is a cool-weather plant that typically blooms in the late spring or early summer.

To harvest curly dock leaves, the leaves can be carefully picked from the plant by hand. The leaves can be eaten raw in salads or cooked in a variety of dishes, such as soups, stews, and sautés. Curly dock leaves are a good source of vitamins A and C, as well as minerals such as iron and calcium.

Curly dock seeds can also be harvested and used as a grain substitute. The seeds can be dried, roasted, and ground into a flour, which can be used in baking or as a thickener in soups and stews. Curly dock seeds are a good source of protein and fiber, and have a nutty, slightly sour flavor.

Curly dock has a number of potential health benefits. It is rich in antioxidants, helping protect the body from damage caused by free radicals. Research suggests curly dock may be anti-inflammatory and have potential benefits for the digestive system.

To prepare and eat curly dock, the leaves should be washed and can be eaten raw or cooked. The leaves have a slightly sour, lemony flavor that pairs well with other ingredients, such as garlic and onions. Curly dock seeds can be harvested, dried, and ground into flour, or can be roasted and eaten as a snack.

CURRANT

Currants (Ribes spp.) are shrubs that produce small, tart berries that are commonly used for making jams, jellies, and other food items. There are several species of currant, including red, black, and white currants, and they are native to many parts of the world.

Currants can be easily identified by their leaves, which are simple and lobed, and by their clusters of small, round berries. The berries are typically red, black, or white, depending on the species, and they are tart and slightly sweet.

Currants grow in a variety of habitats, including forests, meadows, and along the edges of rivers and streams. They prefer cool, moist conditions and are often found in areas with moderate to high rainfall.

Currants are in season from late spring to early summer, and the berries can be harvested during this time. The berries are rich in vitamins and minerals, including vitamins C and K, and potassium and antioxidants. Currants are also a good source of fiber and have been shown to have several health benefits, including reducing inflammation and improving heart health.

To harvest currants, simply pick the berries from the bush. Be sure to only harvest currants from areas that have not been treated with pesticides or other chemicals. The berries can be eaten raw or cooked, and they are often used to make jams, jellies, syrups, and other food items.

When preparing currants for eating, it is important to wash them thoroughly to remove any dirt or debris. The berries can be eaten raw or cooked, and they are often used in baked goods, such as pies, tarts, and muffins. They can also be added to smoothies, juices, and other drinks for a healthy and delicious boost of flavor.

DANDELION

Dandelion is a hardy, herbaceous perennial that is native to Europe and Asia, but it has been widely naturalized in other parts of the world, including North America. It is a highly nutritious plant that has been used for food and medicine for thousands of years.

Dandelion can be easily identified by its basal rosette of deeply lobed, green leaves and its bright yellow flowers that bloom in the spring and summer. The plant produces a distinctive, round, puffball-like structure that contains many small, seeds that are dispersed by the wind.

Dandelion grows in a variety of habitats, including lawns, fields, and waste ground. It is a hardy plant that is suited to a wide range of growing conditions and can be found throughout North America.

When harvesting dandelion, it is best to gather the leaves when they are young and tender, before the plant begins to flower. The leaves can be harvested by cutting or breaking them from the plant, taking care not to damage the plant or other nearby leaves.

Dandelion is a highly nutritious plant that is a good source of vitamins, minerals, and antioxidants. It is also rich in dietary fiber, and it has been shown to have anti-inflammatory, digestive, and liver-protective benefits.

Dandelion can be used in a variety of ways, including as a leafy green, a substitute for lettuce in salads, or as a cooked green, similar to spinach or kale. The roots can also be roasted and ground to make a coffee substitute, and the flowers can be used to make wine or added to salads.

DAYLILY

Daylily is a herbaceous perennial plant that is native to Asia, but it has been widely cultivated and naturalized in other parts of the world, including North America. It is a highly nutritious plant that has been used for food and medicine for thousands of years.

Daylily can be easily identified by its tall, upright growth habit, its long, narrow leaves, and its large, bright yellow or orange flowers that bloom in the spring and summer. The plant produces large, edible, fleshy bulbs that are similar in taste and texture to a cross between a potato and an onion.

Daylily grows in a variety of habitats, including gardens, meadows, and waste ground. It is a hardy plant that is suited to a wide range of growing conditions and can be found throughout North America.

When harvesting daylilies, it is best to gather the bulbs when they are young and tender, before the plant begins to flower. The bulbs can be harvested by digging around the base of the plant, taking care not to damage the plant or other nearby bulbs.

Daylilies are a highly nutritious plant that is a good source of vitamins, minerals, and antioxidants. They are also low in calories and have been shown to have anti-inflammatory, digestive, and liver-protective benefits.

Daylilies can be used in a variety of ways, including as a vegetable, a substitute for potatoes or onions in recipes, or as a base for soups and stews. The flowers can also be used to make tea, or they can be added to salads or used as a garnish.

DOGWOOD

Dogwood (Cornus spp.) is a deciduous shrub or tree that is native to many parts of the world, including North America, Europe, and Asia. It is easily recognized by its showy, white or pink flowers, which are typically in bloom from late spring to early summer, and its distinctive, opposite leaves.

Dogwood grows in a variety of habitats, including forests, meadows, and along the edges of rivers and streams. It is a hardy plant that can grow in a variety of conditions, from full sun to partial shade.

The fruit of the dogwood is edible and is often used for foraging food. The fruit is small and blue-black in color, and it has a slightly tart flavor that is similar to a blueberry. The fruit is in season from late summer to early autumn, and can be harvested during this time.

To harvest the fruit of the dogwood, simply pick the berries from the bush. Be sure to only harvest dogwood fruit from areas that have not been treated with pesticides or other chemicals. The fruit can be eaten raw or cooked, and it is often used to make jams, jellies, syrups, and other food items.

Dogwood fruit is rich in vitamins and minerals, including vitamins C and K, and antioxidants. It is also a good source of fiber and has been shown to have several health benefits, including reducing inflammation and improving heart health.

When preparing dogwood fruit for eating, it is important to wash it thoroughly to remove any dirt or debris. The fruit can be eaten raw or cooked, and it is often used in baked goods, such as pies, tarts, and muffins. They can also be added to smoothies, juices, and other drinks for a healthy and delicious boost of flavor.

ELDERBERRY

Elderberry is a deciduous shrub that is native to Europe and North America. It is a highly valued food source prized for its small, tart to sweet berries.

Elderberry can be easily identified by its tall, shrubby growth habit, its leaves that are pinnately compound, and its clusters of small, white or cream-colored flowers that bloom in the spring. The berries are typically dark blue or black in color and are round, with a distinctive flavor that can be either tart or sweet depending on the variety and growing conditions.

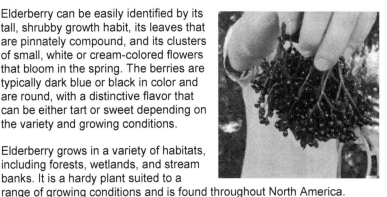

Elderberry grows in a variety of habitats, including forests, wetlands, and stream banks. It is a hardy plant suited to a range of growing conditions and is found throughout North America.

When harvesting elderberries, it is best to pick the berries when they are fully ripe and have a deep blue or black color. The berries can be harvested by gently pinching them from the stem, taking care not to damage the plant or other nearby berries.

Elderberries are a highly nutritious food that is a good source of vitamins, minerals, and antioxidants. They are also low in calories and have been shown to have anti-inflammatory, cardiovascular, and immune-boosting benefits.

Elderberries can be eaten raw, cooked, or baked into a variety of dishes. They can be used to make jams, jellies, syrups, and baked goods, or they can be added to pies, sauces, and other desserts. They can also be dried or frozen for later use.

FIREWEED

Fireweed is a herbaceous perennial plant that is native to the Northern Hemisphere, including North America. It is a highly valued food source, prized for its young shoots, leaves, and flowers.

Fireweed can be easily identified by its tall, upright growth habit, its leaves that are long and narrow, and its large spikes of pink or purple flowers that bloom in the summer and fall. The plant produces long, narrow seed pods that are often used for decoration.

Fireweed grows in a variety of habitats, including forests, meadows, and disturbed areas, such as those created by wildfires, hence its common name "fireweed". It is a hardy plant that is well-suited to a wide range of growing conditions and can be found throughout North America.

When harvesting fireweed, it is best to gather the young shoots and leaves when they are young and tender, before the plant begins to flower. The shoots and leaves can be harvested by cutting or breaking them from the plant, taking care not to damage the plant or other nearby shoots and leaves.

Fireweed is a highly nutritious plant that is a good source of vitamins, minerals, and antioxidants. It is also low in calories and has been shown to have anti-inflammatory, digestive, and immune-boosting benefits.

Fireweed can be used in a variety of ways, including as a leafy green, a substitute for lettuce in salads, or as a tea. The young shoots and leaves can also be used in soups, stews, and stir-fries, or they can be pickled or added to salads. The flowers can be used to make jelly or added to salads for flavor and color.

GARLIC MUSTARD

Garlic mustard is a biennial herb that is native to Europe but has been introduced to North America and other parts of the world as an invasive species. Despite its invasive nature, garlic mustard is considered an edible plant.

Garlic mustard can be easily identified by its basal rosette of green leaves that have a distinctive garlic-like odor, and its tall, upright stems that produce clusters of white flowers in the spring. The leaves, stems, and flowers of the plant are all edible and have a mild garlic flavor.

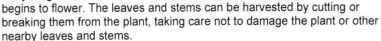

Garlic mustard grows in a variety of habitats, including woodlands, meadows, and disturbed areas. It is a hardy plant suited to a range of growing conditions and can be found throughout North America.

When harvesting garlic mustard, it is best to gather the leaves and stems when they are young and tender, before the plant begins to flower. The leaves and stems can be harvested by cutting or breaking them from the plant, taking care not to damage the plant or other nearby leaves and stems.

Garlic mustard is a highly nutritious plant that is a good source of vitamins, minerals, and antioxidants. It is also low in calories and has been shown to have anti-inflammatory, digestive, and immune-boosting benefits.

Garlic mustard can be used in a variety of ways, including as a leafy green, a substitute for lettuce in salads, or as a cooked green, similar to spinach or kale. The leaves and stems can also be used in soups, stews, and stir-fries, or they can be added to sauces or dips for flavor.

GOOSEBERRIES

Gooseberries (Ribes uva-crispa) are a species of fruit-bearing shrub that is native to Europe and Asia, and is widely cultivated in many parts of the world, including North America.

Gooseberries can be easily identified by their small, green or red fruit, which is surrounded by a thin, papery husk. The shrubs have spiny branches and dark green leaves, and they are commonly found along the edges of forests and in abandoned orchards.

Gooseberries are in season from late spring to early summer, and they can be harvested by picking the fruit from the shrub. When harvesting gooseberries, it is important to only take what you need and to leave some for wildlife and for future harvests.

Gooseberries are rich in vitamins and minerals, including vitamins C and K, and minerals such as potassium and magnesium. They are also a good source of antioxidants and have been shown to have several health benefits, including improving heart health and reducing inflammation.

Gooseberries can be enjoyed fresh, or they can be used in a variety of recipes, including jams, jellies, pies, and baked goods. They can also be frozen or dried for later use. When using gooseberries in cooking, it is important to balance their tart flavor with sweetness, either by adding sugar or by combining them with sweeter fruits.

GRAPE

Grapes (Vitis species) are a well-known fruit that are native to the Northern Hemisphere, including North America. They are a highly valued food source, prized for their sweet, juicy taste.

Grapes are easily identified by their clusters of round to oval-shaped fruit that are typically green, red, or purple in color. They grow on woody vines that can climb up trees or other structures, or they can be trained to grow on trellises or other support systems. The vines produce large, lobed leaves and clusters of small, white or yellow flowers that bloom in the spring.

Grapes grow in a variety of habitats, including forests, meadows, and along river banks. They are a hardy plant suited to a wide range of growing conditions and can be found throughout North America.

When harvesting grapes, it is best to pick the fruit when it is fully ripe and has a deep, rich color. The fruit can be harvested by gently pinching it from the stem, taking care not to damage the vine or other nearby fruit.

Grapes are a highly nutritious fruit that is a good source of vitamins, minerals, and antioxidants. They are also low in calories and have been shown to have anti-inflammatory, cardiovascular, and immune-boosting benefits.

Grapes can be eaten raw, cooked, or baked into a variety of dishes. They can be used to make juices, wines, and baked goods, or they can be added to salads, sauces, and other desserts. They can also be dried or frozen for later use.

GRASS

Grass is a common plant that grows in many different environments around the world. While it is not typically considered a food source for humans, there are certain types of grass that can be foraged.

Edible grasses can be identified by their slender, green leaves, which grow in dense clumps or as individual blades. The plant may also produce seeds that can be consumed.

Edible grasses can be found in a variety of environments, including meadows, fields, and prairies. They may bloom at different times of the year depending on the species, but many grasses bloom in the summer or fall.

To harvest edible grasses, the leaves or seeds can be carefully picked by hand. The leaves can be eaten raw in salads or cooked in a variety of dishes, such as stir-fries and soups. Some species of grass, such as wheatgrass, can also be juiced and consumed for their nutritional benefits.

Edible grasses are a good source of fiber, vitamins, and minerals, including potassium and vitamin C. They are also low in calories and can help promote healthy digestion.

To prepare and eat edible grasses, they should be washed thoroughly and any tough parts, such as stems, should be removed. The leaves can be eaten raw or cooked, while the seeds can be roasted and consumed as a snack or used as a grain substitute in baking.

HAZELNUTS

Hazelnuts are the edible nuts produced by the hazel tree (Corylus avellana), which is native to Europe and Asia, but is also found in other parts of the world, including North America. They are small, round nuts encased in a hard, brown shell and mature in the fall.

Hazelnuts can be easily identified by their distinctive, round shape and their shell, which is covered in a hard, brown outer layer. The trees are commonly found in forests and along the edges of rivers and streams, and they prefer moist, well-drained soils.

Hazelnuts are in season from late summer to early autumn, and they can be harvested by shaking the tree or picking them up from the ground. The nuts have a sweet, nutty flavor.

Hazelnuts are rich in vitamins and minerals, including vitamins B and E, and minerals such as magnesium and potassium. They are also a good source of healthy unsaturated fats, fiber, and protein.

To prepare hazelnuts for eating, it is important to remove the shell and then roast or boil the nuts to remove any bitterness. The nuts can then be eaten as a snack, added to baked goods, or used in cooking. Try using hazelnuts in savory dishes such as roasted vegetables or in sweet dishes such as cakes and cookies for a unique and delicious foraging experience!

HUCKLEBERRY

Huckleberries (Vaccinium species) are a type of berry that is native to North America and is prized for its sweet, tart flavor and versatility in cooking. Huckleberries grow on low shrubs or small trees and are widely distributed throughout the United States, especially in the western states.

Huckleberries can be identified by their small, round to oval-shaped fruit that is typically blue or black in color. The shrubs or trees that they grow on are usually less than 6 feet tall and have green, leathery leaves. Huckleberries typically ripen in late summer to early fall and are often found in forested areas, such as the understory of coniferous forests.

When harvesting huckleberries, it is best to pick the fruit when it is fully ripe and has a deep, rich color. The fruit can be harvested by gently pinching it from the stem, taking care not to damage the shrub or other nearby fruit.

Huckleberries are a highly nutritious fruit that is a good source of vitamins, minerals, and antioxidants. They are also low in calories and have been shown to have anti-inflammatory, cardiovascular, and immune-boosting benefits.

Huckleberries can be eaten raw, cooked, or baked into a variety of dishes. They can be used to make jams, jellies, and syrups, or they can be added to baked goods, such as muffins and pancakes. They can also be dried or frozen for later use.

JACKFRUIT

Jackfruit (Artocarpus heterophyllus) is a tropical tree that is native to South and Southeast Asia, but is now widely cultivated in other tropical regions, including South and Central America, Africa, and the Caribbean. Jackfruit is prized for its large, juicy fruit that has a sweet, slightly tangy flavor.

Jackfruit can be easily identified by its large, oblong-shaped fruit that can weigh up to 100 pounds or more. The fruit is covered in a green, spiky exterior, and when ripe, has a yellow or orange flesh that is fragrant and sweet. The tree itself is a large, fast-growing species that can reach up to 40 feet in height and produces large leaves and clusters of small, yellow flowers.

Jackfruit grows best in tropical regions with high temperatures and abundant rainfall. It is a hardy plant that is well-suited to a wide range of growing conditions.

When harvesting jackfruit, it is best to pick the fruit when fully ripe with a deep, rich color. The fruit can be harvested by cutting it from the tree, taking care not to damage the tree or other nearby fruit.

Jackfruit is a highly nutritious fruit that is a good source of vitamins, minerals, and antioxidants. It is low in calories and has been shown to have anti-inflammatory, digestive, and immune-boosting benefits.

Jackfruit can be used in a variety of ways, including as a fresh fruit, in baked goods, or in savory dishes. The ripe fruit can be eaten raw or added to smoothies and other drinks, while the unripe fruit can be used in curries and stews. The seeds of the jackfruit can also be roasted and eaten as a snack.

LAMB'S QUARTERS

Lamb's quarters (Chenopodium album) is an annual herb that is native to Europe and Asia, but is now widely distributed throughout the world, including North America.

Lamb's quarters can be easily identified by its green, triangular leaves that are covered in a powdery white film, and its tall, upright stems that produce small, green flowers in the summer. The leaves, stems, and flowers of the plant are all edible and have a mild, nutty flavor.

Lamb's quarters grows in a variety of habitats, including gardens, fields, and disturbed areas.

When harvesting lamb's quarters, it is best to gather the leaves and stems when they are young and tender, before the plant begins to flower. The leaves and stems can be harvested by cutting or breaking them from the plant, taking care not to damage the plant or other nearby leaves and stems.

Lamb's quarters is a highly nutritious plant that is a good source of vitamins, minerals, and antioxidants. It is also low in calories and has been shown to have anti-inflammatory, digestive, and immune-boosting benefits.

Lamb's quarters can be used in a variety of ways, including as a leafy green, a substitute for spinach in salads, or as a cooked green, similar to spinach or kale. The leaves and stems can be used in soups, stews, and stir-fries, or added to sauces or dips for flavor.

MAPLE

Maple (Acer spp.) is a genus of deciduous trees that is native to many parts of the world, including North America, Europe, and Asia. It is known for its distinctive leaves, which are usually lobed and have a bright, vibrant color in the fall, and its sweet sap.

Maple trees can be easily identified by their leaves, which are typically lobed and have a bright, vibrant color in the fall. The trees are commonly found in forests and along the edges of rivers and streams, and they prefer moist, well-drained soils.

Maple sap is harvested from the tree in the late winter or early spring, when the temperatures are just above freezing during the day and below freezing at night. To harvest the sap, a small hole is drilled into the tree and a tap is inserted. The sap then drips out of the tap and is collected in a container. The sap is then boiled down to concentrate the sugars and make maple syrup.

Maple syrup is a rich source of vitamins and minerals, including vitamins B and C, and minerals such as calcium and potassium. It is also a good source of antioxidants and has been shown to have several health benefits, including reducing inflammation and improving heart health.

Maple syrup can be used as a sweetener in a variety of foods and drinks, including pancakes, waffles, coffee, and tea. It can also be used in baking and cooking to add a unique, sweet flavor to dishes. When purchasing maple syrup, it is important to look for pure, natural syrup and to avoid syrups that have been mixed with other sweeteners or additives.

MINT

Mint (Mentha spp.) is a genus of aromatic, perennial herbs that is native to many parts of the world, including Europe, Asia, and North America.

Mint can be easily identified by its fragrant leaves, which are usually bright green and have a serrated edge. The plants are commonly found in moist, well-drained soils and can often be found growing along the edges of streams or in damp meadows.

Mint is typically harvested in the summer or early fall, when the leaves are at their peak of flavor and fragrance. To harvest the leaves, simply cut off a sprig of the plant, taking care to remove any yellow or damaged leaves. The leaves can then be used fresh or dried for later use.

Mint is rich in vitamins and minerals, including vitamins A and C, and minerals such as iron and calcium. It is also a good source of antioxidants and has been shown to have several health benefits, including improving digestion, reducing inflammation, and freshening breath.

Mint can be used in a variety of ways, including as a flavoring in tea, as a garnish in cocktails, or as an ingredient in baked goods, sauces, and dressings. When using mint in cooking, it is important to use it sparingly, as its strong flavor can easily overpower other ingredients. Fresh mint leaves can also be enjoyed as a refreshing snack, simply washed and eaten whole or torn into pieces.

MOREL MUSHROOMS

Morel mushrooms (Morchella spp.) are a genus of edible fungi that is highly prized for its distinctive, spongy cap and rich, nutty flavor. They are found in many parts of the world, including North America, Europe, and Asia, and they typically grow in forests and along the edges of streams.

Morel mushrooms can be easily identified by their distinctive, spongy cap,

which is usually brown or black in color and has a honeycomb-like texture. The stems are white and have a slightly hollow center.

Morel mushrooms are in season from late spring to early summer, and they can be harvested by picking them from the ground. When harvesting morels, it is important to only take what you need, as over-harvesting can negatively impact the health of the ecosystem and future harvests.

Morel mushrooms are a good source of protein, fiber, and vitamins, including vitamins B and D. They are also a rich source of antioxidants and have been shown to have several health benefits, including reducing inflammation and improving heart health.

Morel mushrooms can be enjoyed in a variety of ways, including sautéed, grilled, or baked. They can also be used in soups, sauces, and stews for a unique, nutty flavor. When preparing morels, it is important to clean them thoroughly and to cook them thoroughly to destroy any harmful bacteria or parasites that may be present.

NETTLE

Nettle (Urtica dioica) is a perennial herb that is native to Europe, Asia, and North America, but is now widely distributed throughout the world.

Nettle can be easily identified by its green, heart-shaped leaves that are covered in small, stinging hairs, and its tall, upright stems that produce small, green flowers in the spring and summer. The leaves, stems, and flowers of the plant are all edible, but the stinging hairs must be removed before consumption.

Nettle grows in a variety of habitats, including forests, meadows, and along river banks.

When harvesting nettle, it is best to gather the leaves and stems when they are young and tender, before the plant begins to flower. The leaves and stems can be harvested by cutting or breaking them from the plant, taking care to wear gloves or use tongs to avoid the stinging hairs.

Nettle is a highly nutritious plant that is a good source of vitamins, minerals, and antioxidants. It is also low in calories and has been shown to have anti-inflammatory, digestive, and immune-boosting benefits.

Nettle can be used in a variety of ways, including as a leafy green, a tea, or as a cooked green, similar to spinach or kale. The leaves and stems can also be used in soups, stews, and stir-fries, or they can be added to sauces or dips for flavor. The dried leaves can be used to make a tea, which is said to have a variety of health benefits, including improving digestion and reducing inflammation.

OSTRICH FERN

Ostrich fern, or Matteuccia struthiopteris, is a type of fern that is found throughout North America. It is known for its distinctive taste and is used as a delicacy in many different types of cuisine.

Ostrich fern can be identified by its tall, feathery fronds that resemble ostrich plumes. The plant typically grows in shady, moist areas, such as forests and stream banks, and can be found in many different

environments. Ostrich fern fronds emerge in the early spring and can be harvested from April to May.

To harvest ostrich fern, the fiddleheads can be carefully plucked from the plant by hand. Fiddleheads are the young, coiled fronds that emerge from the ground in the early spring. Ostrich fern fiddleheads have a distinctive, nutty flavor and can be prepared in a variety of ways, such as sautéed, steamed, or pickled. Ostrich fern fiddleheads are a good source of vitamins and minerals, including vitamin C and iron.

Ostrich fern fiddleheads also have potential health benefits. They have been used traditionally as a natural remedy for a range of health conditions, including respiratory issues, digestive problems, and anemia. Some research has also suggested that ostrich fern fiddleheads may have antioxidant and anti-inflammatory properties.

To prepare and eat ostrich fern fiddleheads, the fiddleheads should be washed and any brown papery scales should be removed. The fiddleheads can be cooked in a variety of dishes, such as stir-fries and pasta dishes. They should be cooked thoroughly to avoid any potential gastrointestinal issues.

OX-EYE DAISY

Ox-eye daisy, or Leucanthemum vulgare, is a wildflower that is found throughout North America. It is known for its distinctive, white, daisy-like flowers and is used as a natural remedy for a variety of health conditions.

Ox-eye daisy can be identified by its tall stems, which can reach up to three feet in height, and its distinctive, white, daisy-like flowers with yellow centers. The plant typically grows in open fields and meadows, and can be found in many different environments. Ox-eye daisy blooms in the summer, typically from June to August.

To harvest ox-eye daisy, the flowers can be carefully plucked from the plant by hand. The flowers can be used fresh or dried for later use in teas or tinctures. Ox-eye daisy flowers are known for their potential digestive benefits, and as a natural remedy for a range of digestive issues, including stomach upset and indigestion. Ox-eye daisy also has potential health benefits for the respiratory system.

The flowers can be used in a variety of dishes, such as salads or as a garnish. The flowers have a slightly bitter taste, and can be used to add unique flavor to a range of dishes.

PECAN

Pecans are the nuts produced by the pecan tree (Carya illinoinensis), which is native to North America.

Pecans can be easily identified by their large, oblong shape and their shell, which is covered in a hard, brown outer layer. The trees are commonly found in forests and along the edges of rivers and streams, and they prefer moist, well-drained soils.

Pecans are in season from late summer to early autumn, and they can be harvested by shaking the tree or picking them up from the ground. The nuts have a sweet, nutty flavor and are often roasted or used in baking.

Pecans are rich in vitamins and minerals, including vitamins E and B, and minerals such as magnesium and potassium. They are also a good source of healthy unsaturated fats, fiber, and protein.

To prepare pecans for eating, it is important to remove the shell and then roast or boil the nuts to remove any bitterness. The nuts can then be eaten as a snack, added to baked goods, or used in cooking. Try using pecans in savory dishes such as roasted vegetables or in sweet dishes such as cakes and cookies for a unique and delicious foraging experience!

PENNYCRESS

Pennycress, or Thlaspi arvense, is an edible plant that is found in North America.

Pennycress can be identified by its small, white flowers and its seed pods, which resemble tiny, flat pennies. The plant typically grows in open fields, along roadsides, and in disturbed areas, and can be found in many different environments. Pennycress blooms in the spring, typically from April to June.

To harvest pennycress, the leaves and seed pods can be carefully plucked from the plant by hand. The leaves and seed pods can be eaten raw or cooked, and have a slightly peppery taste. Pennycress is known for its potential health benefits, including its anti-inflammatory and antioxidant properties.

Pennycress has been used in traditional medicine to treat a range of health conditions, including respiratory issues and digestive problems. Some research has also suggested that pennycress may have potential benefits for the cardiovascular system, including lowering cholesterol levels.

To prepare and eat pennycress, the leaves and seed pods should be washed and any brown or yellow parts should be removed. They can be used in a variety of dishes, such as salads and soups, and can be added to stir-fries and other dishes for a unique flavor.

PINEAPPLE WEED

Pineapple weed, or Matricaria discoidea, is a small, aromatic herb that is found throughout North America. It is known for its pineapple-like aroma and is used as a natural remedy for a variety of health conditions.

Pineapple weed can be identified by its small, round flower heads that resemble miniature pineapples. The plant typically grows in disturbed areas, such as roadsides and fields, and can be found in many different environments. Pineapple weed blooms in the summer, typically from June to September.

To harvest pineapple weed, the flower heads can be carefully plucked from the plant by hand. The flower heads can be eaten raw or cooked, and have a sweet, fruity flavor with a hint of spice. Pineapple weed is known for its potential digestive benefits, and has been used as a natural remedy for digestive issues, including stomach upset and indigestion.

Pineapple weed also has potential health benefits for the respiratory system. It has been used to soothe coughs and other respiratory ailments, and may help to reduce inflammation in the lungs.

To prepare and eat pineapple weed, the flower heads should be washed and any stems or leaves should be removed. The flower heads can be eaten raw in salads or cooked in a variety of dishes, such as stir-fries and soups. Pineapple weed can also be used to make tea, either alone or in combination with other herbs.

PINE

Pine (Pinus species) is a type of coniferous tree that is native to many parts of the world, including North America. The seeds, also known as pine nuts, from certain species of pine trees are edible.

Pine trees can be easily identified by their tall, conical shape and their needles, which grow in clusters of two to five on each branch. The cones of pine trees are also distinctive, and the cones of the species that produce edible seeds are usually large and woody.

Pine trees grow in a variety of habitats, including forests, mountains, and along river banks. They are hardy trees that are well-suited to a wide range of growing conditions and can be found throughout North America.

When harvesting pine nuts, it is best to gather the cones when they are mature and have begun to dry out. The cones can be harvested by breaking them open to reveal the seeds, which are usually found in the center of the cone.

Pine nuts are a highly nutritious food that is a good source of healthy fats, protein, and vitamins and minerals. They have been shown to have a variety of health benefits, including improving heart health, reducing inflammation, and supporting weight management.

Pine nuts can be used in a variety of ways, including as a snack, in baked goods, or as a topping for salads and pasta dishes. They can also be used in savory dishes, such as pesto and sauces, to add a nutty flavor and texture.

PLANTAIN

Plantain, or Plantago major, is a common herb that is found in many parts of the world.

Plantain can be identified by its long, narrow leaves with parallel veins and small, inconspicuous flowers that grow on spikes. The plant typically grows in disturbed areas, such as roadsides, meadows, and lawns, and can be found in many different environments.

To harvest plantain, the leaves can be carefully plucked from the plant by hand. The leaves can be used fresh or dried for later use in teas or tinctures. Plantain leaves are known for their anti-inflammatory and wound-healing properties and have been used as a natural remedy for a range of health conditions, including respiratory issues, digestive problems, and skin irritations.

Plantain also has potential health benefits for the respiratory system. It has been used to soothe coughs and other respiratory ailments, and may help to reduce inflammation in the lungs.

To prepare and eat plantain, the leaves can be eaten raw in salads or cooked in a variety of dishes, such as stir-fries and soups. Plantain leaves are a good source of vitamins and minerals, including vitamin A and calcium.

PRICKLY PEAR CACTUS

Prickly pear cactus, also known as Opuntia, is a type of cactus that is commonly found in arid and semiarid regions around the world.

The prickly pear cactus can be easily recognized by its flat, paddle-shaped stems (known as "nopales") that are covered in small, spiny thorns. These stems can grow up to 3 feet long and can be a vibrant green or blue-green

color. The cactus also produces colorful, edible fruit that can be red, orange, or yellow, and is covered in small, hair-like thorns.

Prickly pear cactus is native to Mexico and the southwestern United States, but also found in other warm, dry regions of the world, such as South America, Africa, and the Middle East. It is a hardy plant that grows in a variety of soil types, including sandy and rocky soils.

The prickly pear cactus typically blooms in the late spring or early summer, producing beautiful, showy flowers in shades of pink, red, or yellow. These flowers are followed by the fruit, which ripens in late summer and early fall.

To harvest the fruit, it's important to wear thick gloves and use tongs or a pair of pliers to carefully remove it from the cactus. The fruit can then be washed and eaten raw or cooked. It is a good source of fiber, vitamins, and minerals, including vitamin C, magnesium, and potassium. Research has also suggested that prickly pear cactus may have anti-inflammatory and blood sugar-lowering properties.

To prepare and eat prickly pear cactus, the thorns must be removed first. This can be done by carefully scraping the fruit with a sharp knife or peeling it with a vegetable peeler. The fruit can be eaten raw, sliced and added to salads, or cooked and used in a variety of dishes, such as jams, jellies, and sauces. Nopales can also be cooked and used in savory dishes such as tacos, soups, or stir-fries.

PURSLANE

Purslane (Portulaca oleracea) is an annual herb that is native to the Mediterranean region, but is now widely distributed throughout the world, including North America.

Purslane can be identified by its small leaves that are fleshy and plump, and its prostrate stem that grows close to the ground. The plant produces yellow or yellow-orange flowers in the summer. The leaves, stems, and flowers of the plant are edible.

Purslane grows in a variety of habitats, including gardens, fields, and disturbed areas.

When harvesting purslane, it is best to gather the leaves and stems when they are young and tender, before the plant begins to flower. The leaves and stems can be harvested by cutting or breaking them from the plant, taking care not to damage the plant or other nearby leaves and stems.

Purslane is a highly nutritious plant that is a good source of vitamins, minerals, and antioxidants. It is also low in calories and has been shown to have anti-inflammatory, digestive, and immune-boosting benefits.

Purslane can be used in a variety of ways, including as a leafy green, a salad ingredient, or as a cooked green, similar to spinach or kale. The leaves and stems can also be used in soups, stews, and stir-fries, or they can be added to sauces or dips for flavor.

RASPBERRY

Raspberry (Rubus idaeus) is a deciduous shrub that is native to Europe and Asia, but is now widely cultivated and naturalized throughout the world, including North America.

Raspberry plants can be easily identified by their prickly stems and leaves, and their sweet, juicy fruit that grows in clusters on the tips of the branches. The fruit is typically red, but can also be black or golden, depending on the variety.

Raspberry plants grow in a variety of habitats, including forests, meadows, and along river banks.

When harvesting raspberries, it is best to gather the fruit when it is fully ripe and has turned a deep, rich color. The fruit can be harvested by gently pulling it from the stem, taking care not to damage the plant or other nearby fruit.

Raspberries are a highly nutritious fruit that is a good source of vitamins, minerals, and antioxidants. They are also low in calories and have been shown to have anti-inflammatory, digestive, and immune-boosting benefits.

Raspberries can be used in a variety of ways, including as a snack, in baked goods, or as a topping for yogurt, cereal, or ice cream. They can also be used in sauces, jams, and jellies, or they can be frozen for later use.

ROSE HIPS

Rose hips (Rosa species) are the fruit of the rose plant and are often foraged for food. They are the small, round, fleshy structures that remain after the petals have fallen off the rose.

Rose hips can be easily identified by their bright red or orange color and their distinctive shape, which is similar to a small, rounded berry. They grow on the tips of the branches of the rose plant and are typically harvested in the fall, after the first frost has occurred.

Rose hips grow in a variety of habitats, including gardens, parks, and along river banks. They are hardy plants that are well-suited to a wide range of growing conditions and can be found throughout North America.

When harvesting rose hips, it is best to gather them when they are fully ripe and have turned a deep, rich color. The hips can be harvested by gently pulling them from the stem, taking care not to damage the plant or other nearby hips.

Rose hips are a highly nutritious food that is a good source of vitamins, minerals, and antioxidants. They are also low in calories and have been shown to have anti-inflammatory, digestive, and immune-boosting benefits.

Rose hips can be used in a variety of ways, including as a snack, in teas, or in preserves and jams. They can also be used in baked goods, such as muffins and bread, or they can be added to soups, stews, and sauces for flavor.

SALMONBERRY

Salmonberry, or Rubus spectabilis, is a delicious and nutritious berry that is native to the Pacific Northwest region of North America.

Salmonberry can be identified by its thorny canes, palmate leaves, and small, pink flowers that bloom in the spring. The berries themselves are typically orange or reddish in color and have a sweet, slightly tart flavor. Salmonberry bushes can be found in wooded areas, particularly in moist and shaded environments.

To harvest salmonberries, the ripe berries can be carefully plucked from the bush by hand. Salmonberries are a good source of vitamins and minerals, including vitamin C and potassium.

Salmonberry also has a number of potential health benefits. It has been used traditionally as a natural remedy for a range of health conditions, including digestive issues, respiratory infections, and skin conditions. Some research has also suggested that salmonberry may have antioxidant and anti-inflammatory properties.

To prepare and eat salmonberry, the berries should be washed and any stems or leaves should be removed. The berries can be eaten raw or cooked, while the seeds can be strained out and used in jams or sauces. Salmonberry can also be used to make tea or other drinks.

SALSIFY

Salsify, also known as Tragopogon porrifolius, is an edible plant that is commonly found in Europe and North America.

Salsify can be identified by its long, thin, tapering leaves and large, yellow flowers that resemble dandelion flowers. The plant grows in dense clusters and typically blooms in the late spring and early summer. It can be found in many different environments, including meadows, fields, and along roadsides.

To harvest salsify roots, the plant should be carefully dug up from the ground using a garden fork or similar tool. The roots can then be cleaned and cooked in a variety of dishes, such as soups, stews, and roasts. Salsify roots are a good source of vitamins and minerals, including vitamin C and iron.

Salsify also has a number of potential health benefits. It has been used traditionally as a natural remedy for a range of health conditions, including digestive issues, liver problems, and respiratory infections. Some research has also suggested that salsify may have antioxidant and anti-inflammatory properties.

To prepare and eat salsify greens, the leaves should be washed and any tough parts, such as the stems, should be removed. The leaves can be eaten raw in salads or cooked in a variety of dishes, such as stir-fries and sautés. Salsify greens are a good source of vitamins and minerals, including vitamin A and calcium.

SERVICEBERRY

Serviceberry, also known as Amelanchier, is a small tree or shrub that produces edible berries. It is commonly found in North America and has been used for food and medicine for centuries.

Serviceberry can be identified by its smooth, gray bark and oval-shaped leaves with toothed edges. The tree or shrub produces small, white or pink flowers in the spring, which are followed by clusters of small, purple-black berries in the summer. The berries are similar in appearance to blueberries and are typically 1/4 to 1/2 inch in diameter.

Serviceberry can be found in a variety of habitats, including forests, meadows, and along riverbanks. It is a hardy plant that can grow in a variety of soil types and climates.

To harvest serviceberries, the berries can be carefully picked from the tree or shrub using your fingers or a small tool. The berries can be eaten fresh, used in jams and jellies, or dried for later use. Serviceberries are a good source of fiber, vitamins, and antioxidants.

Serviceberry also has a number of potential health benefits. It is rich in anthocyanins, which are powerful antioxidants that can help protect the body from damage caused by free radicals. Some research has also suggested that serviceberry may have anti-inflammatory properties and potential benefits for heart health.

To prepare and eat serviceberries, they should be washed and can be eaten fresh or used in a variety of dishes. Serviceberries can be used in pies, muffins, and other baked goods, as well as in jams, jellies, and sauces. They have a sweet, slightly tart flavor that is similar to blueberries.

SHEPHERD'S PURSE

Shepherd's purse is a leafy green plant that is commonly found in temperate regions around the world.

Shepherd's purse can be identified by its distinctive heart-shaped leaves and small, white flowers that resemble miniature daisies. The plant grows in dense clusters and typically blooms in the spring and fall. It can be found in many different environments, including meadows, fields, and along roadsides.

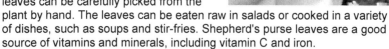

To harvest shepherd's purse leaves, the leaves can be carefully picked from the plant by hand. The leaves can be eaten raw in salads or cooked in a variety of dishes, such as soups and stir-fries. Shepherd's purse leaves are a good source of vitamins and minerals, including vitamin C and iron.

Shepherd's purse also has a number of potential health benefits. It has been used traditionally as a natural remedy for a range of health conditions, including digestive issues, menstrual cramps, and respiratory infections. Some research has also suggested that shepherd's purse may have antioxidant and anti-inflammatory properties.

To prepare and eat shepherd's purse, the leaves should be washed and any tough parts, such as the stems, should be removed. The leaves can be eaten raw or cooked, while the flowers can be used to add color and flavor to salads or other dishes. Shepherd's purse can also be used in tea or tinctures for its medicinal properties.

SIBERIAN MINER'S LETTUCE

Siberian Miner's Lettuce, also known as Claytonia sibirica or Spring Beauty, is a leafy green plant that is commonly found in the northern hemisphere, including North America and Asia.

Siberian Miner's Lettuce can be identified by its distinctive heart-shaped leaves and small, delicate white flowers. The plant grows in dense clusters and typically blooms in the spring. It prefers to grow in moist environments, such as near streams or in shady areas.

To harvest Siberian Miner's Lettuce leaves, the leaves can be carefully picked from the plant by hand. The leaves can be eaten raw in salads or cooked in a variety of dishes, such as soups and stir-fries. Siberian Miner's Lettuce leaves are a good source of vitamins and minerals, including vitamin C and potassium.

Siberian Miner's Lettuce also has a number of potential health benefits. It is rich in antioxidants, which can help protect the body from damage caused by free radicals. Some research has also suggested that Siberian Miner's Lettuce may have anti-inflammatory properties and potential benefits for heart health.

To prepare and eat Siberian Miner's Lettuce, the leaves should be washed and any tough parts, such as the stems, should be removed. The leaves can be eaten raw or cooked, while the flowers can be used to add color and flavor to salads or other dishes.

SORREL

Sorrel (Rumex acetosa) is a perennial herb native to Europe, but is now widely distributed throughout the world.

Sorrel can be easily identified by its arrow-shaped leaves that are tart and acidic in taste, and its tall stem that can grow up to three feet in height. The plant produces small, greenish-yellow flowers in the summer. The leaves, stems, and flowers of the plant are all edible.

Sorrel grows in a variety of habitats, including fields, forests, and along river banks. It is a hardy plant that is well-suited to a wide range of growing conditions.

When harvesting sorrel, it is best to gather the leaves when they are young and tender, before the plant begins to flower. The leaves can be harvested by cutting or breaking them from the plant, taking care not to damage the plant or other nearby leaves and stems.

Sorrel is a highly nutritious plant that is a good source of vitamins, minerals, and antioxidants. It is low in calories and has been shown to have anti-inflammatory, digestive, and immune-boosting benefits.

Sorrel can be used in a variety of ways, including as a leafy green, a salad ingredient, or as a cooked green, similar to spinach or kale. The leaves can also be used in soups, stews, and sauces for flavor.

SOW THISTLE

Sow thistle, also known as Sonchus oleraceus, is a leafy green plant that is commonly found in temperate regions around the world.

Sow thistle can be identified by its spiky, lobed leaves and small, yellow flowers that resemble dandelion flowers. The plant grows in dense clusters and typically blooms in the summer. It can be found in many different environments, including meadows, fields, and along roadsides.

To harvest sow thistle leaves, the leaves can be carefully picked from the plant by hand. The leaves can be eaten raw in salads or cooked in a variety of dishes, such as soups and stir-fries. Sow thistle leaves are a good source of vitamins and minerals, including vitamin C and iron.

Sow thistle also has a number of potential health benefits. It has been used traditionally as a natural remedy for a range of health conditions, including digestive issues, liver problems, and respiratory infections. Some research has also suggested that sow thistle may have antioxidant and anti-inflammatory properties.

To prepare and eat sow thistle, the leaves should be washed and any tough parts, such as the stem and spiky edges, should be removed. The leaves can be eaten raw or cooked, while the flowers can be used to add color and flavor to salads or other dishes. Sow thistle can also be used in tea or tinctures for its medicinal properties.

SPRUCE TIPS

Spruce tips (Picea species) are the new growth shoots of spruce trees, and are often foraged for food. They are a highly nutritious and flavorful food that are rich in vitamins, minerals, and antioxidants.

Spruce trees can be easily identified by their conical shape, their needle-like leaves, and their distinctive pine scent. The new growth shoots, or tips, are typically a bright, light green color and are found at the very top of the tree.

Spruce trees grow in a variety of habitats, including forests and along river banks. They are hardy trees that are well-suited to a wide range of growing conditions.

When harvesting spruce tips, it is best to gather them when they are young and tender, before they have had a chance to mature and harden. The tips can be harvested by cutting or breaking them from the tree, taking care not to damage the tree or other nearby growth shoots.

Spruce tips are a highly nutritious food that is a good source of vitamins, minerals, and antioxidants. They are also low in calories and have been shown to have anti-inflammatory, digestive, and immune-boosting benefits.

Spruce tips can be used in a variety of ways, including as a snack, in teas, or in preserves and jams. They can also be used in baked goods, such as muffins and bread, or they can be added to soups, stews, and sauces for flavor.

STINGING NETTLE

Stinging nettle (Urtica dioica) is a perennial herb that is native to Europe and Asia, but is now widely distributed throughout the world, including North America.

Stinging nettle can be easily identified by its serrated leaves and its distinctive stinging hairs that cover the leaves and stems. The plant produces small, greenish-yellow flowers in the spring and summer. The leaves, stems, and flowers of the plant are all edible, but must be handled with care to avoid the stinging hairs.

Stinging nettle grows in a variety of habitats, including fields, forests, and along river banks. It is a hardy plant that is well-suited to a wide range of growing conditions.

When harvesting stinging nettle, gather the leaves and stems when they are young and tender, before the plant begins to flower. The leaves and stems can be harvested by cutting or breaking them from the plant, taking care to wear gloves to protect from the stinging hairs. Once the leaves and stems are cooked or dried, the stinging hairs lose their potency and can be safely consumed.

Stinging nettle is a highly nutritious plant that is a good source of vitamins, minerals, and antioxidants. It is also low in calories and has been shown to have anti-inflammatory, digestive, and immune-boosting benefits.

Stinging nettle can be used in a variety of ways, including as a leafy green, a soup ingredient, or as a tea. The leaves and stems can also be dried and used in a variety of other dishes.

STRAWBERRY

Strawberries (Fragaria species) are a small, juicy, and sweet fruit that is often foraged for food. They grow on low-growing plants that are native to North America, as well as other parts of the world.

Strawberries can be easily identified by their small size, bright red color, and characteristic conical shape. The plants produce white flowers in the spring and the fruit is typically ripe in the summer.

Strawberries grow in a variety of habitats, including fields, forests, and along river banks. They are hardy plants that are well-suited to a wide range of growing conditions and can be found throughout North America.

When harvesting strawberries, it is best to wait until the fruit is fully ripe and has turned a bright red color. The fruit can be harvested by gently pulling it from the plant, taking care not to damage the plant or other nearby fruit.

Strawberries are a highly nutritious fruit that is a good source of vitamins, minerals, and antioxidants. They are also low in calories and have been shown to have anti-inflammatory, digestive, and immune-boosting benefits.

Strawberries can be used in a variety of ways, including as a snack, in fruit salads, or as a topping for yogurt, cereal, or ice cream. They can also be used in baked goods, such as muffins and bread, or they can be made into jams, jellies, and preserves.

THIMBLEBERRY

Thimbleberry, or Rubus parviflorus, is a wild berry that is native to North America. It is closely related to raspberries and blackberries and is known for its sweet, juicy flavor.

Thimbleberry can be identified by its large, soft, and fuzzy leaves that are shaped like a thimble, as well as its large, white or pink flowers that bloom in the late spring and early summer. The plant typically grows in shaded areas, such as forests and woodland edges.

To harvest thimbleberries, the ripe berries can be carefully plucked from the bush by hand. Thimbleberries are a good source of vitamins and minerals, including vitamin C and potassium.

Thimbleberry also has a number of potential health benefits. It has been used traditionally as a natural remedy for a range of health conditions, including digestive issues, respiratory infections, and skin conditions. Some research has also suggested that thimbleberry may have antioxidant and anti-inflammatory properties.

To prepare and eat thimbleberries, they should be washed and any stems or leaves should be removed. The berries can be eaten raw or cooked, while the seeds can be strained out and used in jams or sauces. Thimbleberries can also be used to make tea or other drinks.

THISTLE

Thistle (Cirsium species) is a group of plants that are native to North America, as well as other parts of the world.

Thistle can be easily identified by its spiny leaves and stems, as well as its large, showy flowers. The plants are typically found in fields, along roadsides, and in disturbed areas, and they are well-suited to a wide range of growing conditions.

When harvesting thistle, it is best to gather the leaves and stems when they are young and tender, before the plant begins to flower. The leaves and stems can be harvested by cutting or breaking them from the plant, taking care to wear gloves to protect from the spines. Once the leaves and stems are cooked or dried, the spines lose their potency and can be safely consumed.

Thistle is a highly nutritious plant that is a good source of vitamins, minerals, and antioxidants. It is also low in calories and has been shown to have anti-inflammatory and digestive benefits.

Thistle can be used in a variety of ways, including as a leafy green, a soup ingredient, or as a tea. The leaves and stems can also be dried and used in a variety of other dishes.

WALNUTS

Walnuts are the edible nuts produced by the walnut tree (Juglans spp.), which is native to many parts of the world, including North America, Europe, and Asia.

Walnuts can be easily identified by their large, round shape and their husk, which is covered in a green, leathery outer layer. The trees are commonly found in forests and along the edges of rivers and streams, and they prefer moist, well-drained soils.

Walnuts are in season from late summer to early autumn, and they can be harvested by shaking the tree or picking them up from the ground. The nuts have a rich, nutty flavor and are often roasted or used in baking.

Walnuts are rich in vitamins and minerals, including vitamins B and E, and minerals such as magnesium and potassium. They are also a good source of healthy unsaturated fats, fiber, and protein.

To prepare walnuts for eating, it is important to remove the husk and then roast or boil the nuts to remove any bitterness. The nuts can then be eaten as a snack, added to baked goods, or used in cooking. Try using walnuts in savory dishes such as roasted vegetables or in sweet dishes such as cakes and cookies for a unique and delicious foraging experience!

WATERCRESS

Watercress is a leafy green plant that grows in freshwater streams and springs.

Watercress can be identified by its small, round leaves, which are a vibrant green color. The plant grows in dense clusters and has small, white flowers that bloom in the summer. Watercress thrives in cool, flowing water and can be found in many regions of the world.

To harvest watercress, the leaves can be carefully picked from the plant by hand. The leaves can be eaten raw in salads or cooked in a variety of dishes, such as soups and stir-fries. Watercress leaves are a good source of vitamins A and C, as well as minerals such as calcium and iron.

Watercress also has a number of potential health benefits. It is rich in antioxidants, which can help protect the body from damage caused by free radicals. Some research has also suggested that watercress may have anti-inflammatory properties and potential benefits for heart health.

To prepare and eat watercress, the leaves should be washed and can be eaten raw or cooked. The leaves have a slightly bitter, peppery flavor that pairs well with other ingredients, such as citrus and goat cheese. Watercress can also be used in juicing and smoothies for an extra boost of nutrition.

WILD CARROT

Wild carrot (Daucus carota), also known as Queen Anne's lace, is a biennial plant that is native to Europe and Asia, but is now widely distributed throughout the world, including North America.

Wild carrot can be easily identified by its lacy white flowers that resemble umbrellas and its fern-like leaves. The plant produces white flowers in the second year of its life cycle and the seeds are typically ripe in the summer.

Wild carrot grows in a variety of habitats, including fields, forests, and along roadsides. It is a hardy plant that is well-suited to a wide range of growing conditions.

When harvesting wild carrot, it is best to gather the seeds when they are ripe and have turned brown. The seeds can be harvested by breaking the dried seed heads and shaking out the seeds, taking care to avoid the bristles on the seed heads.

Wild carrot is a highly nutritious plant that is a good source of vitamins, minerals, and antioxidants. It is also low in calories and has been shown to have anti-inflammatory and digestive benefits.

Wild carrot seeds can be used in a variety of ways, including as a spice, in baking, or as a tea. The seeds have a slightly bitter, earthy flavor and are often used to flavor breads, crackers, and other baked goods.

WILD GARLIC

Wild garlic (Allium vineale), also known as wild onion, is a perennial plant that is native to North America and is widely distributed throughout the United States and Canada.

Wild garlic can be easily identified by its distinctive garlic-like aroma, its long, narrow leaves, and its delicate white flowers. The plant typically flowers in the spring and the leaves and bulbs can be harvested throughout the growing season.

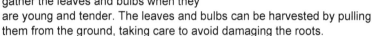

Wild garlic grows in a variety of habitats, including fields, forests, and along roadsides. It is a hardy plant that is well-suited to a wide range of growing conditions.

When harvesting wild garlic, it is best to gather the leaves and bulbs when they are young and tender. The leaves and bulbs can be harvested by pulling them from the ground, taking care to avoid damaging the roots.

Wild garlic is a highly nutritious plant that is a good source of vitamins, minerals, and antioxidants. It is also low in calories and has been shown to have anti-inflammatory and digestive benefits.

Wild garlic can be used in a variety of ways, including as a green, in soups and stews, or as a seasoning. The leaves and bulbs have a strong garlic flavor and can be used to add flavor to a variety of dishes.

WILD GINGER

Wild ginger, or Asarum canadense, is a wild herb that is native to North America. It is known for its pungent, spicy aroma and is used as a flavoring in many different types of cuisine.

Wild ginger can be identified by its heart-shaped leaves and brownish-purple flowers that bloom in the spring. The plant typically grows in wooded areas and can be found in many different environments, including forests and hillsides.

To harvest wild ginger, the roots can be carefully dug up from the ground using a garden fork or similar tool. The roots can then be cleaned and used as a flavoring in a variety of dishes, such as soups, stews, and sauces. Wild ginger contains a compound called aristolochic acid, which is toxic in large amounts. Use in moderation and avoided by pregnant women.

Wild ginger also has a number of potential health benefits. It has been used traditionally as a natural remedy for a range of health conditions, including nausea, headaches, and arthritis. Some research has also suggested that wild ginger may have anti-inflammatory and pain-relieving properties.

WILD LETTUCE

Wild Lettuce (Lactuca virosa) is a species of flowering plant that is native to Europe and Asia and is widely naturalized in many parts of the world, including North America. It is known for its bitter, milky sap and its mild, lettuce-like flavor, and it has been used for centuries for its medicinal properties, especially for pain and inflammation relief.

Wild Lettuce can be easily identified by its tall, slender stems and its large, slightly serrated leaves. The plant has small, yellow flowers that are arranged in a tight cluster at the top of the stem. Wild Lettuce is commonly found along the edges of forests and in fields, and it prefers well-drained soils.

Wild Lettuce is in bloom from late spring to early summer, and the sap can be harvested and used for medicinal purposes. To extract the sap, simply cut a stem near the base of the plant and gently squeeze the sap out of the stem. When harvesting Wild Lettuce, it is important to only take what you need and to leave some for wildlife and for future harvests.

The sap of Wild Lettuce contains a number of active compounds, including lactucin and lactucopicrin, which are believed to have pain-relieving and anti-inflammatory properties. The sap can be applied directly to the skin for pain and inflammation relief, or it can be ingested in small doses for medicinal purposes.

WILD ONION

Wild onion (Allium spp.), also known as wild garlic, is a perennial plant that is native to North America and is widely distributed throughout the United States and Canada.

Wild onion can be easily identified by its distinctive onion-like aroma, its long, narrow leaves, and its delicate white flowers. The plant typically flowers in the spring and the leaves and bulbs can be harvested throughout the growing season.

Wild onion grows in a variety of habitats, including fields, forests, and along roadsides.

When harvesting wild onion, it is best to gather the leaves and bulbs when they are young and tender. The leaves and bulbs can be harvested by pulling them from the ground, taking care to avoid damaging the roots.

Wild onion is a highly nutritious plant that is a good source of vitamins, minerals, and antioxidants. It is also low in calories and has been shown to have anti-inflammatory and digestive benefits.

Wild onion can be used in a variety of ways, including as a green, in soups and stews, or as a seasoning. The leaves and bulbs have a strong onion flavor and can be used to add flavor to a variety of dishes.

WILD PLUMS

Wild Plums (Prunus spp.) are a genus of deciduous trees or shrubs that are native to many parts of the world, including North America.

Wild plums can be easily identified by their small, round fruit that is typically purple or red in color. The trees or shrubs are commonly found in forests, along the edges of rivers and streams, and in abandoned orchards, and they prefer well-drained soils.

They are in season from late summer to autumn, and can be harvested by picking the fruit from the tree or shrub. The fruit has a sweet, juicy flesh and a small pit in the center.

Wild plums are rich in vitamins and minerals, including vitamins C and K, and minerals such as potassium and magnesium. They are also a good source of dietary fiber and antioxidants, and have been shown to have several health benefits, including improving heart health and reducing inflammation.

Wild plums can be eaten fresh, used in baked goods, or made into jams, jellies, and sauces. They can also be dried or frozen for later use. When harvesting wild plums, it is important to only take what you need and to leave some for wildlife and for future harvests.

WILD RASPBERRY

Wild raspberry (Rubus idaeus) is a deciduous shrub that is native to North America.

Wild raspberry can be easily identified by its prickly stems, its dark green leaves, and its clusters of small, red, juicy berries. The plant typically flowers in the spring and the berries are ready for harvesting in the late summer and early fall. Wild raspberry grows in a variety of habitats, including forests, meadows, and along roadsides.

When harvesting wild raspberry, it is best to wait until the berries are fully ripe and have turned a deep red color. The berries can be gently plucked from the bush, taking care to avoid the prickly stems.

Wild raspberry is a highly nutritious plant that is a good source of vitamins, minerals, and antioxidants. It is also low in calories and has been shown to have anti-inflammatory and digestive benefits.

Wild raspberry can be used in a variety of ways, including fresh, in preserves, baked goods, or as a sweetener for drinks and smoothies. The sweet, juicy berries have a unique flavor that is both tart and sweet and can be used to add flavor to a variety of dishes.

WILD RICE

Wild rice is a type of grass that grows in shallow water or along the edges of lakes, rivers, and wetlands. It is an edible plant that has been a staple food for many Native American tribes for centuries.

Wild rice can be identified by its tall, slender stalks that can grow up to 10 feet tall. The plant has long, narrow leaves that grow in pairs along the stem. The most distinctive feature of wild rice is its distinctive seed head, which is a long, slender cluster of small, brownish-black seeds.

Wild rice is native to North America and is primarily found in the Great Lakes region. It grows in shallow water, in places such as marshes, swamps, and the edges of lakes and rivers. Wild rice is a cool-weather plant that blooms in the late summer or early fall.

To harvest wild rice, the seed heads must be collected and dried. This can be done by gently bending the seed heads over a container and shaking them to release the seeds. The seeds can then be spread out on a clean, dry surface and left to air dry. Once dry, the seeds can be cooked and eaten.

Wild rice is a nutritious food high in protein, fiber, and essential vitamins and minerals. It is also a gluten-free grain, making it a great option for people with gluten sensitivities. Research has suggested that wild rice may have anti-inflammatory and antioxidant properties, as well as potential benefits for heart health.

To prepare wild rice, the seeds should be rinsed and then cooked in water or broth until they are tender. Wild rice can be used in a variety of dishes, such as soups, stews, and salads. It has a nutty, earthy flavor that pairs well with other ingredients, such as mushrooms, nuts, and dried fruit.

WILD ROSE

Wild rose (Rosa spp.) is a deciduous shrub that is native to North America and is widely distributed throughout the United States.

Wild rose can be identified by its prickly stems, its bright green leaves, and its clusters of fragrant, showy flowers. The plant typically flowers in the spring and early summer and the hips, which are the fruit of the plant, are ready for harvesting in the late summer and fall.

Wild rose grows in a variety of habitats, including forests, meadows, and along roadsides. It is a hardy plant that is well-suited to a wide range of growing conditions.

When harvesting wild rose hips, it is best to wait until they are fully ripe and have turned a deep red or orange color. The hips can be gently plucked from the bush, taking care to avoid the prickly stems.

Wild rose hips are a highly nutritious plant that is a good source of vitamins, minerals, and antioxidants. They are low in calories and have been shown to have anti-inflammatory and digestive benefits.

Wild rose hips can be used in a variety of ways, including fresh, in preserves, baked goods, or as a tea. The sweet, juicy hips have a unique flavor that is both tart and sweet and can be used to add flavor to a variety of dishes.

WILD SWEET PEA

Wild sweet pea, also known as Lathyrus odoratus, is a flowering vine that produces edible pods and seeds.

Wild sweet pea can be identified by its delicate, fragrant flowers, which range in color from pink to purple to white. The plant produces long, slender pods that contain edible seeds. The seeds are similar in appearance to garden peas, but are smaller and have a nuttier, slightly sweet flavor.

Wild sweet pea is a hardy plant that can grow in a variety of habitats, including meadows, fields, and along roadsides. It typically blooms in the late spring or early summer.

To harvest wild sweet pea pods, the pods can be carefully picked from the plant by hand. Wild sweet pea pods are a good source of protein and fiber, and have potential health benefits for the immune system and digestion. However, it's important to note that other parts of the wild sweet pea plant, such as the leaves and stems, contain toxic compounds and should not be consumed.

To prepare and eat wild sweet pea pods, they should be washed and any tough parts, such as the stem and ends, should be removed. The pods can be eaten raw in salads or cooked in a variety of dishes, such as stir-fries and risottos. Wild sweet pea seeds can also be dried and used as a grain substitute in baking.

WILD TURNIP

Wild turnip, also known as wild rutabaga or wild mustard, is a root vegetable that is commonly found in wooded areas and fields throughout North America.

Wild turnip can be identified by its distinctive white or yellow roots, which are bulbous and can grow up to several inches in diameter. The plant also produces long, narrow leaves with jagged edges that grow from a central stem. Wild turnip typically blooms in the spring or early summer, producing small, yellow flowers.

Wild turnip is a hardy plant that can grow in a variety of soil types and climates. To harvest wild turnip, the roots must be carefully dug up from the ground using a trowel or similar tool. The roots can then be washed and used in a variety of dishes, such as soups, stews, and roasted vegetables. Wild turnip roots are a good source of fiber, vitamin C, and other essential nutrients.

Wild turnip also has a number of potential health benefits. It is rich in antioxidants, which help protect the body from damage caused by free radicals. Research has also suggested that wild turnip may have anti-inflammatory properties and may be beneficial for heart health.

To prepare and eat wild turnip, the roots should be washed and peeled, then cooked until tender. They can be roasted, boiled, or mashed, and seasoned with herbs and spices to enhance their flavor. The leaves of the wild turnip plant can also be eaten and are often used in salads or as a garnish.

WILD VIOLETS

Wild violet (Viola spp.) is a small, herbaceous plant that is native to North America.

Wild violets can be easily identified by their heart-shaped leaves and their showy, purple flowers that bloom in the spring.

Wild violets grow in a variety of habitats, including forests, meadows, and along roadsides. They are a hardy plant well-suited to a wide range of growing conditions.

When harvesting wild violets, it is best to pick the leaves and flowers when they are young and tender. They can be gently plucked from the plant and used fresh or dried for later use.

Wild violets are a nutritious plant that is a good source of vitamins and minerals, including vitamins A and C, calcium, and iron. They also have a number of health benefits, including antioxidant and anti-inflammatory properties.

Wild violets can be used in a variety of ways, including fresh in salads, as a garnish, or as a tea. They have a slightly bitter and tangy flavor that is well-suited to a variety of dishes.

WILLOW

Willow is a tree that is commonly found throughout North America, Europe, and Asia. It is a member of the Salix genus and is known for its medicinal properties.

Willow can be identified by its long, narrow leaves with serrated edges and slender branches. The tree typically grows near water sources, such as rivers, lakes, and wetlands. Willows typically bloom in the early spring, producing small, yellow or green flowers.

To harvest willow bark, the bark can be carefully stripped from the tree using a knife or similar tool. The bark can be dried and used to make tea or tinctures. Willow bark is known for its anti-inflammatory and pain-relieving properties and has been used as a natural remedy for a range of health conditions, including headaches, fever, and arthritis.

Willow also has potential health benefits for the skin. It has been used to soothe sunburn, rashes, and other skin irritations. The leaves can also be used to make a tea that is said to have a calming effect on the nervous system.

WOOD SORREL

Wood sorrel (Oxalis spp.) is a small, herbaceous plant that is native to North America.

Wood sorrel can be identified by its clover-like leaves, which are green and have a heart-shaped appearance. The leaves of the plant have a sour, lemony flavor and are often used as a garnish or added to salads.

Wood sorrel grows in a variety of habitats, including forests, meadows, and along roadsides. It is a hardy plant well-suited to a wide range of growing conditions.

When harvesting wood sorrel, it is best to pick the leaves when they are young and tender. They can be gently plucked from the plant and used fresh or dried for later use.

Wood sorrel is a nutritious plant that is a good source of vitamins and minerals, including vitamins A and C, calcium, and iron. It also has a number of health benefits, including antioxidant and anti-inflammatory properties.

Wood sorrel can be used in a variety of ways, including fresh in salads, as a garnish, or as a tea. Its sour, lemony flavor is suited to a variety of dishes and adds a unique flavor to salads and other dishes.

WILD YAM

Wild yam, also known as Dioscorea, is a vine that is commonly found in tropical and subtropical regions around the world.

Wild yam can be identified by its distinctive heart-shaped leaves, which grow in pairs along the vine. The plant also produces long, cylindrical tubers that can grow up to several feet long. Wild yam typically blooms in the summer, producing small, greenish-white flowers.

Wild yam is native to Africa, Asia, and the Americas, and can be found in a variety of habitats, including forests, meadows, and along riverbanks. It is a hardy plant that grows in a variety of soil types.

To harvest wild yam, the tubers must be carefully dug up from the ground using a trowel or similar tool. The tubers can then be washed and used in a variety of dishes, such as stews, soups, and stir-fries. Wild yam tubers are a good source of fiber, vitamins, and minerals, including vitamin C, potassium, and manganese.

Wild yam also has a number of potential health benefits. It is rich in antioxidants, which can help protect the body from damage caused by free radicals. Some research has also suggested that wild yam may have anti-inflammatory and pain-relieving properties, as well as potential benefits for hormonal health.

To prepare and eat wild yam, the tubers should be washed and peeled, then cooked until tender. They can be roasted, boiled, or mashed, and seasoned with herbs and spices to enhance flavor. Wild yam can be used in traditional medicine practices, such as Ayurveda and Chinese medicine, where it is made into teas or tinctures.

YARROW

Yarrow (Achillea millefolium) is a perennial herb native to North America and commonly found in meadows, fields, and roadsides.

Yarrow can be easily identified by its feathery leaves and clusters of small, white or yellow flowers that bloom in the summer. The leaves of the plant have a slightly bitter, aromatic flavor and are often used as a garnish or added to salads.

Yarrow grows in a variety of habitats, including meadows, fields, and along roadsides. It is a hardy plant that is well-suited to a wide range of growing conditions and is often found in dense colonies.

When harvesting yarrow, it is best to pick the leaves when they are young and tender. They can be gently plucked from the plant and used fresh or dried for later use.

Yarrow is a nutritious plant that is a good source of vitamins and minerals, including vitamins A and C, calcium, and iron. It also has a number of health benefits, including antimicrobial and anti-inflammatory properties.

Yarrow can be used in a variety of ways, including fresh in salads, as a garnish, or as a tea. Its slightly bitter, aromatic flavor is well-suited to a variety of dishes and adds a unique flavor to salads and other dishes.

YELLOW DOCK

Yellow dock (Rumex crispus) is a perennial herb native to North America and commonly found in meadows, fields, and roadsides.

Yellow dock can be easily identified by its long, narrow leaves that are curly or wavy at the edges and its clusters of small, yellow flowers that bloom in the late summer and early fall.

Yellow dock grows in a variety of habitats, including meadows, fields, and along roadsides. It is a hardy plant that is suited to a wide range of growing conditions and is often found in dense colonies.

When harvesting yellow dock, it is best to pick the leaves when they are young and tender. The roots can be harvested in the fall or early spring, when the plant is dormant. They can be gently plucked from the plant and used fresh or dried for later use.

Yellow dock is a nutritious plant that is a good source of vitamins and minerals, including vitamins A and C, iron, and calcium. It also has a number of health benefits, including antimicrobial and anti-inflammatory properties.

Yellow dock can be used in a variety of ways, including as a vegetable, as a tea, or added to soups and stews. Its slightly bitter, earthy flavor is well-suited to a variety of dishes and adds a unique flavor to soups, stews, and other dishes.

FORAGING FOR INSECTS & BUGS

In an emergency, you might turn to insects or bugs as a protein source when foraging. Here's a list of creepy crawlers that you can find in abundance throughout North America and are safe to eat.

CRICKETS

These insects are a good source of protein and can be found in grassy areas, particularly near water sources.

They can be roasted or fried and eaten as a snack.

GRASSHOPPERS

Similar to crickets, grasshoppers are also a good source of protein and can be found in grassy areas.

They can be roasted, fried, or boiled and used in soups or stews.

ANTS

Ants can be found in most environments and can be eaten raw or cooked.

They have a sour, slightly tangy taste and can be used to flavor dishes or eaten as a snack.

BEETLES

Beetles are also a good source of protein and can be found in many environments.

They can be roasted or fried and eaten as a snack or used in soups or stews.

TERMITES

Termites are a good source of protein and can be found in dead wood.

They can be eaten raw or cooked and have a nutty, slightly sweet flavor.

MEALWORMS

These insects are often used as a pet food, but they can also be eaten by humans.

They can be roasted, fried, or boiled and used in soups or stews.

WAXWORMS

Waxworms are often used as bait, but they can also be eaten by humans.

They have a sweet, slightly nutty flavor and can be roasted or fried and eaten as a snack.

CICADAS

Cicadas are a good source of protein and can be found in wooded areas.

They can be roasted or fried and eaten as a snack or used in soups or stews.